Freezing, Thawing: New & Revised Stories from the Midwest

Other Works by Kyle L. White:
Bear. With Me. {A Field Journal} (2019)
Winter Is Scissors (2018)
Neighbor As Yourself (2016)
Wisconsin River of Grace (Cornerstone Press, 2009)

Freezing, Thawing: New & Revised Stories from the Midwest
Kyle L. White

"I'd rather go through a hurricane than 20-below winters."
—a Floridian who rode out Hurricane Irma,
commenting on her Midwest roots

Contents

Freezing

Do You See Your Neighbors in the Winter?

The evidence suggests the house is inhabited: A light in the window. A flutter in the curtains. The occasional set of tracks in the snow. Garbage cans and recycling bins migrating in and out. Trails are cleared somehow. But, no glimpse of humans. Who knows what's going on over there: Thieves? Terrorists? Coyotes?

This winter I sympathize with the neighbors in those shocking news stories. The stories about the old man who's been found dead in his house. Dead for a year. The neighbors say stuff like, "I think I saw him mowing the lawn a few months ago." Way to go, neighbors.

Everyone's appalled. Really, I mostly just feel better that I am not as slouchy a neighbor as they are. I wasn't sure up 'til now. Thanks, Dead Guy.

But who knows? In this Midwest winter, with 68 inches of snow and 40-below wind chills, maybe all my neighbors are dead. There is no way of knowing, really.

But then, one above-zero day, a sighting. Over the fence, past the snowdrifts, Joe waves. (Or what appears to be Joe. I'll take what I can get, in case I get interviewed.) I wave back. "Do you still live there?" I call. He waves.

"I still live here, too," I call back. "Don't forget, Neighbor."

The Quake of '10

The snowplow crashed through the fence in the backyard and rammed into the back of our house. 4 a.m. on February 10. Or was it a snowplow?

Ka-bam! Clatter, clatter, clatter, clatter! Out-of-balance washing machine. The whole house. All of seven seconds. Maybe.

We awoke with "What the devil was that?!" and leapt from our bed, peering through the windows to the patio door, then the front door. Nothing. Winter winds ripping vinyl siding off the house? Meteorite? Bison stampede?

Other neighbors' houses were hit by snow plows, too, and thieves trying to break in, and airplanes crashing, and—someone said— terrorist attacks. What a morning in little Sycamore, Illinois.

Of course, it was none of these. But never in 20 years would I have guessed what it was, here in northern Illinois. Our neighbor Joe—the science teacher and newly minted meteorologist—guessed it, however, and guessed it right. He sat up thermometer-straight in bed at 4 a.m., according to his wife, Carolyne, and exclaimed, "Earthquake! 4.3!" And then, by her report, he dropped back into a satisfied slumber. Not me.

My brother texted me soon after: "Are you guys OK?"

We were at the epicenter of the news. The *Today Show*. CNN. Facebook. Calls from friends. Aftershocks of sympathy and attention.

"I think we're going to be OK," I said. And we would be, since nary a picture frame had fallen over in the natural disaster. Never mind that the 7.0 earthquake in Haiti, just weeks before, had wiped out about 100,000 people. This would be the topic of conversation for all in Sycamore for the next week: So, did you survive the quake? Did you feel it? What did you think it was? Where were you when it happened?

It was something to call our own. Something unique. Something to talk about, finally, after a long winter. We were important. Apparently we sit on a fault line here in northern Illinois. Who knew? Yes, we were at the center. That is, until the quake got downgraded to a 3.8 and the epicenter got moved three miles east. One Chicagoan commented that they don't even cancel circumcisions during a 3.8 earthquake. I felt robbed.

Oh well, it was a good Midwestern earthquake, wasn't it? Good while it lasted. A minor rumbling predicated by decades of uncomfortable silence. Hidden faults brewing just beneath the surface. Aunts and uncles talking in whispers. Apparently—and this was not reported in the *Daily Chronicle*—the earthquake apologized afterward: "I'm sorry," he said. "I didn't mean it. I was just tired."

"It's OK," we said. "It's no big deal."

And then we drank some coffee and had some zucchini bread. We made circles with the toes of our shoes in the imaginary dust of the linoleum, until someone asked, "So, is there supposed to be snow this week?"

No hard feelings, Earthquake. It's okay. Don't be a stranger.

Tell About a Time You Were Trapped in Bad Weather

Once I was travelling to Washington Island, Wisconsin, with friends. In January.

Washington Island is just off the tip of the Door County peninsula. Imagine Wisconsin as a mitten; Door County is the thumb that juts between Lake Michigan and Green Bay. Why the name Door County? It could be a doorway to recreation, or rest. But it comes from the French, Porte des Mortes. Literally, "the door of the dead." It refers to all the wrecks that have occurred in that passage between the peninsula and the island, but probably has its roots with the local Native Americans.

That fateful January day we were heading to visit friends on the island. In the summer the car ferries run all day, back and forth, on the 45-minute trek. The six mile by six mile island, home to several hundred residents, swells with several thousand in the summers. But in the winter (back then, anyway) there is only one ferry a day. One day it runs to the island. The next day, it returns.

That day it was blowing and frigid, and we set out from the peninsula to the island. As we boarded the ferry, we could see masses of ice pressed up against the shore. Jagged pieces jutting this way and that. Lake Michigan pitching us this way and that as we chugged out into the icy waters. Twenty minutes out, the ferry stopped. We had become frozen into the ice.

The island ferries are not ice cutters, so they can only slide up on top of the ice and crush it underneath. But that day it was too cold, we were too slow, and the way the wind was blowing, we froze in. We were stuck. Trapped. Surrounded by ice. The blue-white chunks pressing into the ferry.

What if help couldn't get to us? How long could we last? There is a story in Washington Island's history, 1935, where part of the high school basketball team plunged into frigid waters while driving across the ice. This is still a deadly stretch. Our thoughts turned to rescue. And survival.

As I tell this story, my friend asks: "Did you have heat?"

"Well, yeah."

"Food and water?" she asks.

"Yeah. I guess."

"Bathrooms?"

"Yeah."

"So, what happened next?"

"Well, the, uh, wind shifted and blew some of the ice out. We made it to the island a few hours late. Actually, four hours late. Crazy, eh?"

"Yeah. So you weren't really in any danger?"

"Well, we could have died, I suppose. Coincidentally. You never know. Life is risky."

"I see. Well, that's quite a story," she says.

"Well, when we were stuck we did see a bald eagle swoop down and snatch a duck out of the water. That's pretty in-your-face danger."

"Yeah."

This friend does not take seriously my harrowing tale. In fact, she blows it out of the water. But it's the best I've got. It is my personal "Wreck of the Edmund Fitzgerald," or as close as I will probably get. I can't help that I'm surrounded by safety belts, guard rails, and front and rear bumpers.

Porte des Mortes, not so much. But I could tell you a hundred tales of Porte d'inconvénients.

Too Much Winter

"You can't get too much winter in the winter," Robert Frost wrote—
and what Robert says is true. The more the better. We need to feel this.
We need to feel the full weight of this glorious season. To reflect in the
darkness. To feel the bitter cold and not shrink back. To trudge
through harsh realities and shake them off afterward. To be invigorated
by lungs full of arctic air. These days we need every chance we can get
to prove our hardiness.

"We need not be casualties of the cold, but conquerors." Amen.
Robert Frost did not write that one. That one I heard on a news
feature about ice fishing, while I was watching television during last
week's cold snap. Indoors. The same place Robert Frost penned the
above quote that I found on the Internet.

The Scandalous Truth About You & Cold Weather

All your talk about how you don't want her coming around. Sealing all your doors and windows. Not going out, just to avoid her. It's all a ruse. You would have to remove five layers just to go number one, but you're not fooling anybody. You can't insulate yourself from love.

"Whatever," you say. "What are you talking about?"

Quit the act. It's obvious to everyone. You're constantly checking to see what she's going to do next. Really, she's all you talk about anymore: When is she coming? How long will she stay? I heard a rumor she'll be here 'til Tuesday. What have you heard?

You stare out the window: What's she doing now? Is she thinking of me?

Grandfather Christmas

We always had to wait. After dinner. After the dishes were done. After dessert. And after singing carols.

You, Grandpa, with your plentitude of slicked back hair and your gray cardigan sweater, pumping away at the console organ. Your hands flowing back and forth across that glorious machine like a conjuring magician. "Santa Claus Is Coming to Town" with the castanets tab engaged. And "Rudolph the Red-Nosed Reindeer" with marimba and your signature falsetto warble, segueing into "Silent Night."

Couldn't anyone else see that fat Scotch Pine with the fat frosted lights being swallowed up in a whirlpool of gifts? Open your eyes, people!

But still we waited. You turned down the rheostat, setting the mood. The Fannie May box of assorted chocolates was passed around in slow motion. Each adult laboring over the description of the chocolates on the box lid, as if it were their last chocolate before lethal injection. As if they were dismantling a bomb: *Do we cut the Raspberry Buttercream wire or the Almond Cluster wire?* Never mind that we just finished three types of pie and Bea's cranberry pudding.

Finally, though, Grandma, the Angel of Mercy—the grandma of "Good Gravy!" and even better stuffing—swoops down with her blessing. An explosion of wrapping paper. A scramble for 9-volt batteries. And it's done.

Then you, Grandpa, stick a stray gift bow on Muffy's head. The dog gets the joke, and she'll play your straight man. And you hand out your final gifts: envelopes. Inside, a savings bond for us grandchildren. Or a hundred dollar bill. We are in awe. We don't talk about what we've seen in the envelope.

And after the envelopes are passed around, you doze off on the plaid couch. Eventually, that's where you stayed. Now, almost 93, Grandpa, your glaucoma keeps you anchored there. The tree has gotten smaller—ceramic on the end table—and you have gotten smaller, too. It has gotten dark. And in your slumber, there is a knock. Here on Christmas Eve at midnight. Not the trumpeting front doorbell, but a knock at the back door, at the porch where good neighbors like Pee Wee Brehm and Doc Fleming were welcomed.

You pull yourself to your feet and feel your way around the back of the couch, past the long-silent organ. "Who's there?" you ask.

"It's me, Dad," calls Uncle Kurt. "Open the door."

Confused, you turn the lock, and step out onto that porch.

"Hi, Dad. Just got in from Mesa." Uncle Kurt helps you put on your rubber galoshes and houndstooth overcoat. You don that brown fur hat on your head, and the leather gloves. You step out into crystalline snow on the deck. Winter air refreshes your lungs.

There, in the moonlight, is Sam the Siamese cat, with her iridescent eyes, being chased by Muffy, who barks, "You better run!" They bound through the snow and into the woods. And you begin to head toward those pines, and the glow of the light on the garage, accompanied by the crunch of snow. You fell here a few years ago, but not tonight.

As you tramp through the woods, you see Uncle Mike on his yellow snowmobile, pulling the sleigh with Grandma in her mink coat, bundled under blankets, waving.

"You're a good woman, Benita," you call out, and wave back.

Up ahead on the road, by the garage, Kathy is taking a walk, like every good family should at Christmas. And, back on the deck, Uncle Mark is having a smoke and a good laugh.

You trudge on, through the pines, hands in pockets. You round the corner to the garage door. But you are halted in your tracks by the small crowd gathered there.

"Hey buddy, watch where you're going," one of the Magi mutters.

Pushing through the sheep, you peer into the garage. Nestled amid the Olds 88, the canoe, and Mike's Kawasaki is a tired St. Joseph who gives you a wink, and Mother Mary who smiles, beckoning you closer to the

Christ Child. But you have no gold, or frankincense, or myrrh. Savings bonds and $100 bills aren't accepted here. All you have is your hat in hand. One of the shepherds nudges you forward: "What are you waiting for?"

God's good joke is on you. Mercy and grace. Who could have guessed? And you laugh your good laugh as you bow down before the Christ. Amen. And, amen.

The Dead, of Winter

Behold: hope has frozen over.

Hark: life has drawn her last bitter breath.

Come: bid a cold farewell to joy.

Winter wonderland has turned to icy wasteland.

Alas, it is over. Sniff. This great and glorious Winter Sabbath has come to an end. The culmination of all things, Christmas Break across Community Unit School District #427, ends with a whimper on this dark, frigid Sunday night.

And a faint sucking noise.

At this very moment, the marrow is being drained from our children's bones. Monday morning is a mocking specter: The Ghost of Christmas-That-Didn't-Last.

The Christmas decorations have all been laid to rest, buried with the other boxes in the basement vault. And you, O Christmas tree, O Christmas tree, what did you ever do to deserve this? To be dressed up as if by a drunken undertaker. Then, to be stripped naked and thrown out the back door to shrink in the arctic air. You, O Christmas tree, who never gave up as much as one needle. You, who drank water, God bless you, like an out-of-control diabetic. You, who were at once both Frasier and fir. You, who were worth all 29 dollars and 99 cents. Plus the tax. God rest your soul.

And Monday morning comes, like a slow-motion winter pileup on I-90.

Sliding.

Braking.

Sliding.

Braking.

Sliding.

Breaking.

There is nothing we motorists can do. It. Is. Inevitable. Bewildered victims everywhere.

"I can't do it. It's too hard. It's too-o-o hard," moans our boy as he rises up from under his covers. A resurrection into the old life.

"But I want to keep sleeping. Five more minutes," pleads our girl.

We have passed over to the other side. That purgatory between Christmas and spring. Where the streets are paved with slush. Where we are robed in wet socks, post-nasal drippings, and Vicks VapoRub. Where every tribe and tongue and nation clears their strep throats and croaks their winter croak: "Who will deliver us? From whence does our help come?"

Draw near, St. Casimir Pulaski—whoever you are—with your curious Monday holiday. Save us! We need you now more than ever. Mount up one more revolution. Make war against this darkness, against the oppressive Superintendent of Schools and his minions. Dethrone him for one more day. (And, if it is not too much to ask, a snow day on the preceding Friday. Or the following Tuesday.)

Lord, hear our prayers. Amen. And, amen.

Winter, No. 2

We are all cutouts in the winter. Shoulders angled up to our ears to block the cold. Our white, construction paper breath lurching upward. We totter stiffly out of our square houses, with triangle roofs and rectangle chimneys. Through angular, shoveled paths. At five o'clock the snipped silhouette trees stand against midnight blue sky. And we teeter back to our homes, open the doors, sigh, then melt and spill into the radiance.

Wisconsin Is Grace

Wisconsin is grace. You know, one of those bridges to the Divine. I don't mean, as some outsiders view it, the PackerCheeseBeer&Brat Cult, which may be more of a sect, or even a denomination if you give it, well, grace. But I mean a genuine gift of God.

My family and I recently had lunch with some friends from L.A., who talked about the California exhibit at Disneyland. They speculated, "What other state could have its own Disney attraction? Like, for instance, who would go to a Wisconsin-themed park?!"

Ha. Ha. Ha.

But, in the front pew of my heart, I raised my hand. It's Wisconsin. My birth home. And the home of my re-birth. Because now that I live in Illinois, when I cross back over the border into God's Country, there is a sigh of relief. A burden lifted. Whether it's Madison, or Devil's Lake, Ephraim, Wisconsin Rapids, or Stevens Point, I could offer you dozens of mental snapshots of Wisconsin, where the light of grace rests just so. Like this Polaroid peel-away photo which has been reframed ever-so-slightly by my revisionist history.

"Mythologized," my brother says.

But we both remember. It's from when I was in kindergarten. I'm the round kid on the left.

"We don't like it here and we don't like you, Mom," we had charged matter-of-factly. We were rebelling against an oppressive regime. Who would've believed it was possible right there in central Wisconsin? Right there under the very noses of the good people of Stevens Point even? We'd had enough of work camp. Enough of sweatshop. Enough of dictatorship. There would be no more cleaning of our rooms. No more gagging while wadding paper towels to extract teepee piles of dog poop from our brown shag carpet. "Why is it my job? I didn't do it!" Which is gross if you think about it.

My brother led the rebellion. He was nine. Four years older and wiser. He knew what was really going on around there: Stalin, Mussolini, Our Mother. We, the proletariat, stood in defiance with our rubber boots, snowmobile suits, and Green Bay Packer stocking caps. Our rebel plan? We went for the heart: "We're running away!"

"Where?" she asked.

"Anywhere but here," we said.

6:00 p.m. Freedom! We scuffed and shuffled down Torun Road. A dark winter night in Wisconsin. Our cheeks were stinging hot, as kamikaze snowflakes dive-bombed our frozen eyelashes.

6:06 p.m. We had walked for hours. But there we were, stalled in our tracks. We had come to that particular spot in the road. On one side, that abandoned gray house. Weathered. Windows broken. Every kid for eight blocks knew it was haunted. On the other side there was a logging road, deep and dark in the woods. My brother remembered, "It made that whole place seem like a black hole that you would get sucked into, and never come back."

We didn't dare walk past it in the daylight, much less on that dreadful night.

"I ain't walkin' past it," he said.

"Me neither. Maybe we should go back," I said.

"Home?! No way!"

We looked back toward where we had made our escape, through the smudge of swarming snowflakes and blurred streetlights.

A double take.

A figure in the gray distance.

We squinted through the dark, through the wet snow. It was coming closer. Someone. Carrying something. A club, in its right hand. Oh yes, it was a club all right! Some cartoon caveman, turkey drumstick club! We were trapped. January sweat. Feet frozen by fear. We shivered between lurking ghosts and a madman stepping up to deliver the Stormin' Gorman Thomas homerun blow. Crack! Over the fence, into the ditch, laying us out like two deep-freeze Ball Park Franks.

Our eyes strained through the dark to identify our winter assailant. The last image we would ever see before . . .

"Mom? Is that you?" (Or, maybe it was like that scratch-and-pop LP we had at home, where Hans Christian Andersen's "Little Match Girl" had only enough light to show her just what she didn't have before she froze to death. Who gives their kids that kind of record?)

But no, it was Mom. And she was carrying two scarves in her right hand.

"Why don't you come back home? We're having Polish sausage for dinner," she offered.

And this is what came out of our mouths: "Okay, Mom."

Okay, Mom. Like it was our bright idea.

We headed for the porch light of home. Rescued. And just like that, ghosts and fear melted like snowflakes in the hand. There was never a word mentioned about our rebel offense. It was grace. Grace wrapped in Polish sausage and applesauce. And, our gospel reading that night was from St. Luke, chapter 15: "But while they were still a long way off, they were spotted and compassion was poured out upon them. Footsteps broke into hot pursuit of them. An embrace and kisses all around. 'Bring out the best scarves and put them on them. And put those mittens-on-a-string on their hands. And warm boots on their feet. Don't forget the plastic bread bag liners to keep those feet dry. And bring the fatted Polish sausage. Let us eat and be merry, for these sons of mine were lost and now they have been found.'" Or something like that.

Amen. And amen.

Wisconsin is grace.

Winter, No. 3

"I'd rather go through a hurricane than 20-below winters."

This is from a Florida friend, who rode out Irma, commenting on her Midwest roots. As a Midwesterner myself, this testimony puffed me up a bit. Despite the legendary niceness and humility of Midwesterners, there is an arrogance when it comes to our winters. Ice. Snow. Winds. Below-zero temps. We won't come out and say it, because pride is a sin, but in our hearts we turn up our noses at the winters of others. And then we feel bad that we did.

Midwestern humility comes from a history of being at the mercy of the land and the weather. Something bigger than us. We still believe we are under a Mystery. There is still space to talk about God in the Midwest.

Midwestern lives are lived as though whistling through a cemetery. In winter, we stock up on food, coffee, firewood, and salt, in hopes that we'll make it through another one. And, when winter mercies come, we stand in awe, in our galoshes. Winter cuts us down to size. That's a good thing. It makes us who we are.

The Wisconsin & Illinois Truce of '07

Imagine this: A half-day of school on Friday; then the weekend; then Lincoln's Birthday on Monday, so no school; and then, waking up Tuesday to 40 mph winds and 6–12 inches of snow! Snow day! Grace upon grace.

My kids' joy spilled over and onto the front yard, into tunnels and forts. It makes a man want to be charitable. Except he has to shovel.

I've always thought Illinois winters were rather Nancy-pants in comparison to the winters I grew up with in central Wisconsin—the atmospheric conditions of northern Illinois being the armpit of the Midwest. But this January and February, Illinois has been showing her testosterone in the meteorological department. Weeks of sub-zero temps and foot-deep snow that sticks around for weeks.

It has felt lately like, well, Wisconsin. Good Lord, I can't believe I'm saying this.

I have spent the better part of 16 years here in northern Illinois defending Wisconsin against the attacks of wounded Bears fans. OK, this is not a difficult outpost to fortify, but I'm always on the defense. The volleys come in two or three ways:

1. "Those dirty Packers."
2. "Ha. Ha. You said 'bubbler,' 'hotdish,' etc."
3. "Geez-o-Pete, why do you guys label your county roads with letters? Like 'WW'?"

And, when they want to bring out the big guns, I hear: "Cheesehead!"

So, as a native Wisconsinite, I will not be taken down by a winter broadside here in Illinois. It would be embarrassing.

Donning my union suit, I trudge out to the driveway. I like the idea of shoveling. I don't like shoveling, but I like the idea of it. The idea of "real work" with my hands (I don't do much of that in my line of work). And, I like the idea of visually completing a task (I don't do much of that in my line of work, either). So after a few thrusts of the shovel blade, I find myself dramatically stretching out my back— "Geez-o-Pete! I'm getting too old for this!"—and kicking the slush build-up off the mud flaps of the Subaru.

It's at that point my neighbor—an Illinoisan—comes up with his truck and plow, and says, "Want me to pull the snow out?"

My eyes narrow and my pulse quickens. My grip tightens around the shovel. *Play it cool, man,* I remind myself.

"How much are you charging?" I ask.

"Nothing," he says.

What is he trying to pull here? I wonder. *Keep your hand on your shovel, boy. Let him see you know how to use it.*

"Yeah? Are you sure?"

"Yeah," he says. *Ingenious,* I marvel, *The Trojan Snow Plow.*

"Then I'd love to have you plow us out!" *What the devil am I saying?!?* And then he did it. He plowed us out. And did I mention, another neighbor came with his snow blower and blew out the end of the driveway when we got 12 inches on December 1 of '06? Can you believe it? These are Illinoisans. I am not kidding.

It was on February 13 of '07 that I decided to stop using my shovel for digging foxholes in this war against my friendly Illinois brothers. Instead, I would use it to build bridges. OK, I am kidding about that. I was not going to go that far. But I had been disarmed, and I would call a truce. I would begin to see the possibility of good in the people of Illinois.

There must be some.

Of course, there is Abraham Lincoln, the great Commander-in-Chief and emancipator, but how long can one state play that trump card? OK, they still can, and they should. And, besides my Snow Removal Neighbors, there are other good Illinois people in my community. My kids for one. Or, two. They were born in Illinois, which is still hard to admit. But they are natives, and I like them.

Besides Abraham Lincoln, my Snow Blowing Neighbors, and my kids, there is my son's barber, Windy. There are a couple beautiful things about Windy. One is that he only gives two types of haircuts: the "Little Boy Haircut," and then the one he gives to me, which looks remarkably similar to the "Little Boy Haircut" on my misshapen head. Yet he wields his combs and clippers with great flair, moving about my son's head like a snake charmer. And at the end of each haircut, he conjures up a piece of bubble gum with sleight of hand, and shows the parent for approval before presenting it to the child. The second beautiful thing about Windy the Barber is that he has no hair. None. I heard it was alopecia. I'm enthralled: a man that ministers to the hair needs of others when he cannot grow any of his own. And, he is from Illinois. We saw a sign in his window not long ago: "Windy has retired after 52 years." We miss him.

The sixth good person that I have found from Illinois, my friend Wendell, told me something about where we live. Wendell was a history and social studies teacher before he retired, and he knows everything about gardening; I tend to believe what he says despite his state residency. He told me, "You know, Kyle, the Wisconsin state line used to extend just south of where we live."

I had that usual eye narrowing and pulse quickening I've experienced when dealing with other Illinoisans. *What is he trying to pull here?* But, I figured, if what he's saying is true about Wisconsin creeping like a glacier, or a receding hairline, into Illinois at one point in history, it explains a lot about Abraham Lincoln, and Windy the Barber, and the three or four other good people I have met so far in the Prairie State. If true, I would extend my truce to at least February 15. I will keep you abreast of my historical and territorial findings, and of the peace process. If, on the other hand, he was not telling the truth, truces are easily broken and my trusty shovel is at the ready.

Winter, No. 4

Know who your friends are in the winter. My first real skiing
experience: a 49-year-old surrounded by 40 9-year-olds. On the bunny
hill. The kids slice and swoosh. Swoosh and slice. Fearless. Joyful.

I zig. Turn. Fall. Zag. Turn. Fall. Embarrassed. Frustrated. The only
dignity is that I have patient, experienced skier friends who help me up
at each Zig. Turn. Fall. Zag. Turn. Fall.

These are those gospel friends, and I am the one who has proven,
repeatedly, that I am unable to use my arms and legs. My friends cut a
hole in the roof of the house and lower me, by their kindness, into the
presence of Jesus: "I say to you, rise, pick up your skis and poles, and
go sit in the chalet."

Amen.

Speed Bumps for Glaciers

It was the year of the speed bump. The year my family ran me over. Twice.

I was five or six, I think. But, I'm always five or six in my revisionist history.

The first incident: Stevens Point. Central Wisconsin winter. Pre-Greenhouse Effect. Back when snow was proud. I stood on a glorious 40-foot-high pile that the thundering snow plows had created at the end of our driveway. Mom, my brother, and my sister were returning from the Thrifty-Mart with groceries, cruising down the salt-white road in our cavernous, margarine-yellow tub of a station wagon. I slid down the snow bank and began to run alongside the car. Chugging white breath, I waved to my brother and sister. They waved back.

Me in my blue-black snowmobile suit, Packer stocking cap, and faux-leather rubber boots, laughing. And, at that point, I grabbed the back door handle. My family kept waving, waving, waving, as I slipped, slipped, slipped, and disappeared under the back tire. *Thump. Thump.* The lumbering wagon rolled over my legs and I was pressed into a stunned, fallen snow angel mold at the end of the driveway. Hot tears and breath flowed.

It was an accident, I'm sure.

"No broken bones," Dr. Sevenich said.

The second incident: Stevens Point. Central Wisconsin summer. Greenhouse humidity. There in the twilight, we three siblings played in our mosquito-preserve front yard, under the maple tree where we had flung my sister's Barbie doll, her neck tied to a shoestring (the Barbie's, not my sister's). My brother chased me on his red bike with that sparkly yellow banana seat and knobby tires. The six-foot orange safety flag wagging and taunting as I laughed and panted. Barefoot, I slipped on the dewy grass. *Thump. Thump.* He ran over my head. Tears and sweat mingled with the fresh tread mark across my face.

It was an accident.

"Nothing broken," Dr. Sevenich said.

If only I had been old enough to see the conspiracy. They rolled me out like Silly Putty, pressed and impressed, being careful not to get any of it on the orange shag carpeting in the living room. And in all of that formative rolling and shaping that took place in Wisconsin, I picked up pieces and bits that are now part of me. Like the time in Wisconsin Rapids, at my grandpa and grandma's house, when I plummeted 20 feet out of that pine, landing hard on my back amid the sand, needles, and roots. Luckily, my grandma called her doctor neighbor to come over and examine my spine. Dr. Fleming was an optometrist, but still, it made me feel better. I guess.

Or there was that time during one of my dad's softball games—bands of kids roamed the park behind the diamonds while the men played slow-pitch—where another kid and I thought up the clever pastime of "Rock Fight." The rules, in case you want to play at home, are simple: 1) choose a rock and a partner; 2) mark off about ten yards between the two of you; 3) take turns throwing your rock 'til you hit your partner; and 4) first one to strike his target wins. I wound up, pitched my rock, and missed. Wide right.

The other kid somehow found a Native American arrowhead in the Golden Sands of Plover, and shot it. In Super Slo-Mo, the projectile found its mark directly between my eyes. Cue the deluge of blood. And, continuing in Super Slo-Mo, I fell backward to the earth in a cloud of dust.

Then came the PA announcement: "Game delay! Don White, your kid is bleeding in the dirt behind the outfield fence." The softball fans booed.

"The beer stand is still open," came the announcer again.

"Yay!" cheered the fans.

It's been over 30 years since the stitches were removed, but I'd still punch that kid in the mouth if I saw him on the street today. The scar is still there.

And I still have the scars from rafting on the Wolf River during a storm in junior high, when my rather large partner fell out the back of our yellow raft going over Boy Scout Falls. The ballast being gone, I was catapulted into the river, where my leg wrenched and wedged between two underwater rocks. I was held down there, steeped in a cloud of bubbles, pressed by the current, filling up on the Wolf. But miraculously, I found myself vomiting water on the river bank. It's the closest I've ever come to biting the dust. Fittingly, it almost happened at the hands of Wisconsin's geology.

Considering all this, I realize I've had an embarrassing number of run-ins with Wisconsin soil. A veritable state tour, including the Kettle Moraine, while mountain biking; the smooth white rocks of Washington Island; the sand beach of Pine Lake in Westfield; the gravel on the shoulders of the roads of Amherst. You name the region, I have a story best left for another time. And, while at first read this appears to be a history of my maladroit life—an outward demonstration of the rocks in my head—it is, below the surface, a testimonial of the irresistible, gravitational pull of Wisconsin. Of God's Country.

All those times spent lying flat on my back in the rich soil of this state, I should've looked up, and looked around, at the grace of my surroundings. Growing up, we don't think much of "place." Or, we think about moving on. But I should've seen the clues; I finally get it now after moving away. I am a human glacier tripping, and stumbling, and sliding through this beautiful state, picking up bits and pieces wherever I go. All magnetic fragments that point True North.

Now that I get it, I no longer fight the pull of this place. Wisconsin, for me, has become reorientation and grace. And my brother still tells the stories of the year I was run over by my family, pressed into the dirt. He still tells the stories of the rock to my head, and the rocks in my head, making and revising our history. And still, I am being smoothed, shaped, and polished in the rock tumbler of Wisconsin. But no need to call Dr. Sevenich, God rest his soul. I get it now.

January 20th

Curving paths up the driveway, along the sidewalk. Under the nose, down the chin. Shoveling. Shaving. The same thing: cutting away to the new, "old familiar" underneath. Making way for smooth travel, and maybe a kiss.

Sure, both have their hazards: the chunk of hidden ice that catches the scraper and rams the handle into your breadbasket, or the occasional bloody nick to the chin. But, in the end, you tap your shovel on the concrete, or rinse your razor in the sink. Either way, you did it, brother.

It is finished.

There's plenty of time to get to work. Plenty of time to never-get-anything-done. This is the only time today you can say: The task is complete. So, lean on your snow shovel. Slap on the aftershave. Survey the job well done: your shoveling & shaving Sabbath.

It is good.

Winter, No. 5

"Chop out the dead wood." That's what one of my journalism professors would say when he wanted us to edit a story.

"Chopping out the dead wood" was the act of cutting out the superfluous for the sake of clarity and space. It is the hardest—yet best—part of writing.

Winter is the edited world. Everything's been stripped away. Down to the black and white. Thus, winter is the best time for editing our stories: Do I like my story? What title would I give it? What do I need to whittle away? What do I still need to say?

Winter Is for Writing

Winter is for writing.

You may say, "I'm not a writer." Or, "I don't have anything to write."

Baloney.

Get a good journal, so you'll take it seriously. Sharpen your pencil, or, as in my case, whittle it sharp with your pocket knife. You'll feel more of an urgency and engagement with the endeavor.

In winter, when it's dark by 4:30 p.m., you may even find it's hard to stop writing.

Write a letter to your grandmother, or to your kids. Everyone likes mail. When I was an elementary school kid I would ask if I had gotten any mail. My mom would say, "Well, did you write anyone a letter?" The First Law of the U.S. Postal Service is that you have to send mail to get mail.

Record today's weather, or the funny exchanges you had with people at work or school. Write your own psalm, or all the jokes you can remember, or a haiku (5-7-5, don't forget).

Imagine, in winter, that you are an Antarctic explorer, like Shackleton. Or an astronaut. Or a bear in and out of torpor. Or imagine you are a sparrow, cheerful in the cold.

You will find, if you write in winter, that you will have accomplished something in these dark days. And it will help you contend against desolate and worrisome thoughts.

Winter is for writing.

December 26

There is a spot on Barber Greene Road in DeKalb, Illinois, that is holy ground. I look for it every time I pass, which is at least four times a day, maybe six. You can't see it. It's just concrete and a gravel shoulder. You'd miss it if you were talking on the phone or texting. But, it's holy ground.

Everyone drives this road on their way to Walmart. Past the municipal airport and cornfields. Nothing to see. Maybe a single-engine airplane ascending from the runway. A truck in the harvested field. But there is a spot about 50 yards west of Somonauk Road. On the north side. It is holy ground.

On December 26, the day after Christmas, I saw it. Turning west onto Barber Greene, I noticed a woman with her car stopped on the shoulder. She was standing in the cold, talking on her cell phone. She looked panicked. What is she doing out here? It's freezing. Is she having car trouble? Ahead, past her car, in the middle of the road, was an SUV turned over, passenger side to pavement. Blown out windows. Glass pieces splayed out south across the road. Yet, still: Is this something I need to stop for? Can I just pull around?

Slowly, across glass and debris, I peered beyond the SUV, and there it was: the burning bush. There she was. Sitting? No. Prone. Face down against cold, gray concrete. Arms and hands stretched above her head to the northeast. Pulling beyond her, I got out of my car and ran toward her, slower than even I run. Boots feeling like astronauts' on the pavement. The wind cutting through that flat, open space from the cold, gray sky. High definition, this figure: outlined, stark. This is not where a woman is supposed to lie prostrate, the day after Christmas.

I found myself stooping as I came toward her. Slower and slower. No sound except for the wind. I know why the woman on her cell phone kept her distance; she knew better than to approach. Radiating about the victim's head, a cardinal-red circle. I curved toward her, and in a hushed voice asked, "Are you okay? Are you okay?" *Please be okay.* My question got caught up in the wind. It was too late to ask. She was not okay. I had nothing to offer her. I should have removed my boots at this spot.

"Don't touch her! Don't touch her!" Two women came running up to the victim and knelt beside her. Ministering.

"I can't find a pulse," one said. They were nurses. I checked the SUV for other passengers. The windshield had a shattered hole, the barrel through which she launched. She had not been wearing a seatbelt. Inside the SUV was a car seat, and a baby bottle, and a stroller. I checked the vehicle, and the road, and the ditches. No baby. Thank you, Jesus.

"Take my keys," one nurse called to me. "There's a blanket in the backseat of my car."

Yes. I ran like an astronaut, retrieving the Mickey Mouse fleece blanket. At that moment I remembered I should pray for this woman.

"She has a pulse," one nurse exclaimed. They turned the woman over, cradling her. No concern over the blood. "I can hear her bones breaking when she breathes."

Maybe I prayed for the wrong thing. There was no recognizing her. She could have been 30 or 50. But I know her name. I know because I had taken to collecting her belongings that were strewn down the road. A purse. A comb. Glasses. Reading glasses. A phone. Prescription bottles revealing her name. I collected them in a bucket from her vehicle.

She did not wake that morning thinking that she would be here on the road after lunch. Other drivers began to stop and look busy. But there was nothing we could do. There we all were, orbiting this woman. Gently collecting her belongings. Some holding her. A woman for whom I wouldn't have given a second thought if I saw her at a stoplight. A woman I might have cursed in my head if she were driving poorly. Cursed her because she was talking on her phone, or impeding my progress. And now, I know her name.

There we all were: afraid, and fragile, and small, and clarified, under a cold, gray sky. All of us, too late.

Later, the police arrived. Even later, an ambulance. When does one leave an accident? When does one leave a burning bush? There is no check-out procedure. No sign-out sheet. I got back in my car and drove to my office. I checked for news updates. She was pronounced dead at the hospital.

There is a spot on Barber Greene Road in DeKalb, Illinois. It is holy ground.

Road to Emmaus

"The ice age is coming . . . ," The Clash sang as we listened to 105.7 WAPL in our room, in the dark. We hitched our blankets up tighter.

The long-range forecast changed that night when our parents climbed the stairs and gathered my younger sister, my older brother, and I in my room.

"Sorry, but it's over," they reported. Promises falling like snow.

I tried to cry hard into my pillow, like I knew I should. Strange how quiet it gets after a snowstorm.

And then they handed us their snowball that we would push uphill and back downhill for the next 40 years. And counting.

Divorce is social distancing without the stay-at-home order: "Who gets us this weekend?"

From the window in that room, growing up, I used to scan the skies. Up past that deeply-rooted eastern white pine to ancient Ursa Major. The Milky Way was a concealing curtain: "Is this all there is? Where are you?"

But then as that glacier began to overtake us, a memory of something my brother said before we fell asleep in that room: "He explained . . . what was said in all the Scriptures concerning [the Christ] . . . . Did not the Messiah have to suffer these things and then enter his glory?" He is the God, not out there somewhere, but the God who suffers here.

As much as I pretended to be sleeping, eyes closed tight, never wanting to believe that my brother was right about anything, the story struck like flint.

Outside, through the parted curtains, icicles on the eaves began to drip, drip, drip away. The chat-chat- chattering of teeth giving way to the snap and whistle of kindling.

Amen. And, amen.

Winter, No. 6

In the winter, to bed, we wear thermal underwear, even union suits. We slumber under flannel sheets, even down comforters. And yet, in the middle of the night, wind skirling out-of-doors, we move our legs, like scissors, to poke one out from under the covers. Right foot, up to knee, periscoping in the cold dark. The same reason we flip to the cool side of the pillow: homeostasis. Balancing the elements. Heat and cold. Equal time for spring and winter. Waking and hibernation.

Right leg as groundhog, counting down the days of winter. About six more weeks.

Winter, No. 7

After the last snow there are two sets of tracks in the powder. The mailman's cut east to west, and the rabbit's cut north to south. The trails intersect in the middle of our front yard.

Maybe the mailman came at his usual time—one o'clock in the afternoon—and the rabbit kept his morning hours. Or maybe they ran into each other at the same time. Who knows? But, if so, did they exchange small talk about the weather, and exchange incoming and outgoing mail?

Rabbit has been awaiting his subscription to *Farmer's Almanac*, and news from his 216 siblings.

Winter, No. 8

If you go for a walk, it doesn't matter what you accomplish the rest of the day—you're already ahead. Winter walks, even more so. You'll have proven your hardiness, chugging along like a steam engine, plowing new paths in the snow. You'll have taken time to ponder, to pray, and to plan. Your winter breath the smokestack of your mind's production. Chug. Chug. Chug. You'll find your day's workload cut in two. After all, thinking is always half the job.

New Year's Day

This morning, January 1, 2015, I am considering subtractions: What needs to change from the year past? And additions: What do I need to start doing? But, to assess myself fairly, I am also considering the question: What should I keep doing?

On the first day of 2015, I am convinced more than ever that my primary calling in life is to turn off that light in the back hallway. I don't know why it's always left on. People using the full-length mirror inside the closet door, or loading and unloading the washer and dryer, probably. Maybe seven times a day I have been faithful to perform the task of flipping the switch to the "off" position. Multiply that by 365 days and it equals 144,000 times per year, approximately.

Like a Keeper of the Grail, I'm not getting a paycheck for it, but I also can't walk away. It is my noble, obsessive-compulsive calling. And if it weren't for the smug feeling of "getting it right" that I enjoy, I would get no recognition at all for this duty.

Little does anyone know that by turning off that light (electricity costs $0.10 per kilowatt hour, the average bulb eats 20 watts, times the 144,000, carry the 1) I am saving my family about $3 over the course of a year. A low estimate. But in a real and holy sense, I "keep the lights on" by, well, keeping them off. So, as I face the resolutions and uncertainties of a new year, one thing is assured: I will not veer from this divine labor. I am Guardian of the Light Switch.

Happy New Year.

Thawing

Spring Break Wisconsin

One does not think of going to Wisconsin for spring break.

But each year at spring break, generous friends from my church allow my family to use their Wisconsin lake home for a week. It is really more than a cottage or a cabin; it is sprawling and luxurious. A lavish gift. Each year we take friends with us, as it's too big for our family of four. We bring friends in case we have to form search parties if someone gets lost in the house.

Our spring break party destination is Door County, Wisconsin. The peninsula between Green Bay and Lake Michigan. Thus, our party beach is covered in eight inches of snow and the lake is frozen over. The bay is dotted with snowmobiles and ice fishermen. We do none of those things. We do nap, however, and read, and watch movies, and hike, and eat. Oh, do we eat. Even our movies are about eating: *Jaws*, the first night. There are baskets full of popcorn, chocolate chip cookies, and Red Vines. And we share meals of wood-oven pizza, grilled salmon, pasta. We all contribute. Starting Monday we will get back to the gym and our diets. But this week, friends crowd around tables and laugh and tease each other.

Napping and eating. Eating and napping. To prevent self-loathing and seam-bursting, one has to go for a walk. Some justification for the next snack and nap: "Well, I did walk for 15 minutes this morning. Before I walked to the fridge."

On one morning walk I have my most satisfying meal. This year, spring break is framed by Palm Sunday and Easter, and across from the lake house, back in the woods, there is an Eastern Orthodox prayer chapel. I stop in every time I am in Door County. It is at the end of a path between two small homes, and this week it is deep in snow. Someone has left a shovel, and I have to clear the steps of the stucco structure; it rises like a lighthouse in the pines.

The heavy wooden doors are held shut on the outside by a rock. I shovel the steps, remove the rock, pull back the doors, and am carried in by heavy, sweet incense. I can see my breath in the chapel. The only furnishings are a lectern and some wrought-iron chairs. An oriental rug on the concrete floor. And there is a curtain that hides an altar. Light comes in from windows up near the ceiling. I am not Eastern Orthodox. My church experience is the furthest thing from it. But this quiet mystery spot is holy ground for me each year.

If I ever saw someone at the prayer chapel, I would confess and apologize for defiling the sanctuary. I don't know what I am doing. Compared to my lecture hall church back home, this Eastern Orthodox chapel is a chemistry lab. I sort through the vials and bottles of incense, the charcoal discs, the elaborate tongs, the beeswax candles. Again, I am sorry, but I light them all up. Piles of jasmine incense atop sparking charcoal discs. A candle. Maybe two. I light the thurible, and all the suspended oil lamps. I want to be clothed in it. I want to walk out smelling like the experience for the rest of the day. Like I'd been somewhere.

So, each morning, I tramp back to the chapel and fire up the slow pyrotechnics and sit in the cold, on an iron chair. And I talk to God—more I just sit—under the gaze of mysterious, severe, alien saints, all who have been somewhere. Like St. John the Well Keeper, St. Moses the Ethiopian, and St. Eulalia of the Snowstorm.

And under the flint watch of the Incarnate God Almighty Himself.

Light radiates about their heads from golden halo discs. And the white smoke wanders up toward the windows.

A couple mornings, when I return from my chapel walk, my wife asks: "What did you learn?"

And I have to say, "Nothing, really. I was just there." Like sitting and being silent with someone who knows you. Not having to think of the next thing to say, or complete an assignment. Being versus doing. Resting under the weight of the mystery, and the welcome. There is holiness, but . . . . And there is welcome.

I confess one more defilement, and it is my best meal. At the back of the chapel there is a turned-down, brown paper grocery bag. Next to it there is a hand-written index card that says: Blessed Bread. Help Yourself. And in the bag there are crumbs and cubes of dried out bread. It's not defilement, I just don't know what it's for, and I do help myself, and I labor to crunch it in my back teeth. It tastes like, well, stale bread, but it makes me feel part of the place. And that is the point, I discover. In the Eastern Orthodox Church, only a portion of the round communion loaf is consecrated by the priest. This is called the "Lamb," and it is Eucharistic. For members. The rest of the loaf is cut up and blessed by the priest. It is for any visitor. It is a sign of welcome.

I finish my time, close the wooden doors, replace the rock, and tramp back through the snow. The incense follows me on my coat, and in my scarf, and in my mittens. And back into our friends' house.

Back at the house we eat and nap. Nap and eat. Later, outside, my friend and I light the charcoal grill for the evening's meal. We talk, and laugh, and are quiet. We take pictures of the golden sunset. We pretend we know what we're doing when it comes to grilling; the smoke rises from the coals. We smell like it when we carry the food inside. We pray a blessing, and a thanksgiving for the meal, and we welcome each other around the table again.

Thaw

We stand on Pebble Beach at Little Sister Bay in Door County, Wisconsin. Under a brooding March sky. Under a shroud of lamenting gray clouds.

We watch the dark waves of Green Bay advance to a rhythmic dirge. We watch them usher down masses of ice that are sick to death of the cold.

"Next, please," call the waves to the ice, dashing them on the rocks. Each chunk choosing a headstone for winter.

Our family stands here at the brink in the cold wind, watching this ceremony with some reverence. Winter giving way to spring. Even death must die. We get front row seats. And a quickening.

My wife, our four-year-old daughter, and I throw white rocks into the waves to try to pick off the ice before it ever reaches shore. Gulls circle. We are Israelites pitching rocks at the retreating Philistines, after David has knocked Goliath out stone cold. "Yeah, you better run!" we yell, after a quick look over our shoulders, and one last check for the giant's pulse.

"You never had a chance!" we laugh.

Our daughter does a victory march, stones clattering in her wake. Our nine-month-old son chants. We are full of life. A blast of northerly wind shakes our bones and causes us to burrow into our coats. But it's only a death rattle. Pretty sure.

Yes, winter still lingers. Cold is all around. We don't deny it can even be beautiful and dignified. We just know it's not the end. Pretty sure.

She doesn't know it today, marching on the beach, but five years from now, our daughter will weep in the chapel foyer at her great-grandmother's funeral. One half of the tears will be for her gentle, grace-filled Grandma Bruch, who wore winter so well. The other half of her tears will be for the bitter realization that everyone she knows will die someday. Her mother, her father, her brother, and all the rest.

"Why do people have to die?" she will choke out. Maybe more than half of her tears will be allotted for that. She doesn't know it today, but this girl will be stunned at the audacity of death. Just like every one of us had been at one time. But her faith-filled great-grandma will go quietly to the brink, with confidence that it is not the end. She will go with a God-given white stone tucked in the pocket of her black dress.

Back at Little Sister Bay, our four-year-old skips and gallops, stooping to examine stones along the way. She knows that she has every good reason for a joyful victory march. And we have every good reason to join her, accompanied by the percussion of ice on the rocks. A gust of wind protests, and we give our coats a hitch out of respect. But back up the road, in the woods, the trillium is signing winter's death certificate. Giants are being felled. Even death is dying.

Letter to a Sump Pump

Dear Sump Pump,

Thank you for your years of service. But let's drop the charade.

Last week, during the relentless spring rainstorms, my wife even referred to you as "that poor thing," with all your *whirr-whoosh-clunking* in a dark corner of the basement. Baloney. You may have fooled her, but I know that each *whirr-whoosh-clunk* is the countdown to betrayal.

Because of you, I live in constant fear in my own home. I can't win. If I *do* hear your *whirr-whoosh-clunk* on a rainy day, it means you are closer to failure, and I closer to the brink of deluge. If I *don't* hear your *whirr-whoosh-clunk*, it means you've taken your proverbial finger out of the literal dam, just to see the world go under. You've done it to us before.

At the first drop of rain I say to my wife, "Shhh! Did you hear the pump kick in?" My wife loves being shushed. I run to the basement door to listen down the stairs, around the furnace, past the golf clubs, into your darkness. "Is that water flowing?" I ask her. "Do you hear laughter down there?"

Whirr-whoosh-clunk.

What other machine requires such attention? But, you're more devil than machine. My friend has an app on his phone that tells him when his sump pump has failed. I think there's even a camera that watches. But what could he do from far away at work or on vacation? If you betrayed us, what could we do? Except take front row seats to watch you destroy our worlds.

Worse are when the thunderstorms roll through while we're sleeping. I awaken, terrified: *What the devil? What if the pump can't keep up, or gives up the ghost? What if the power goes out? Why didn't I get that battery back-up? I'm a fool!* I fly to the basement door at 2 a.m. for the *whirr-whoosh-clunk,* rubber boots and bucket at hand. Two a.m. thunderstorms are always the reckoning hour, and you, Sump Pump, the accuser.

I am making deals with God Almighty in the impending flood, like Louis Zamperini adrift in the ocean: "Just let the pump remain unbroken through this storm and I swear I'll dedicate my whole life to you. Again. Please, God." I am confessing my sins. All of them. From the gluttony of the Taco Bell drive-thru at 9 p.m. last night, to that lustful seventh-grade thought I had about Karen Pronschinske in 1982. And other sins of commission—and more, sins of omission. There are neither atheists in foxholes, nor in sump pits.

"Lord have mercy on me, a sinner, and a slave to this sump pump. Amen."

Whirr-whoosh-clunk.

In the end, though, who could ever trust you, Sump Pump? *You poor thing.* Whatever. You spend your whole life lurking down there under the surface. I stand at the edge of the pit, peering into the dark water. Into my own reflection. Dang you all the way to heck, Sump Pump.

Whirr-whoosh-clunk.

I hate you, Sump Pump; but I need you.

Whirr-whoosh-clunk.

My Life Inside the Bureau

I was let go last week from the Bureau.

After giving my all to this federal institution, I am disheartened. To process my curtailed career, I thought it best to write about it. That is perhaps cliché: Bitter Federal Agent Writes Scathing Memoir. It's the stuff of Harrison Ford films. However, after *Indiana Jones: Kingdom of the Crystal Skull*, I would prefer that my part be played by William H. Macy.

As much as I need to write this down, I'm hesitant. I'm not proud of some of the things I did, and I'm not sure my experiences can be explained in layperson terms. Beyond that, I'm not even sure it's legal to write about it; I swore an oath to uphold something. I think it was the Constitution. So yeah, I got canned by the Bureau of the Census.

The FBI wasn't hiring part-time workers, so you take what you can get. I was hired as an "enumerator," which is Bureau lingo for "the guy who verifies your address." Did you know that a national census is required by the Constitution every ten years? But before the 2010 Census surveys could be mailed to every place where people live, or could live (caves and railroad cars are choices in the manual), the enumerators had to go out like Swine Flu and verify addresses with GPS on hand-held computers. HHCs if you're in the Bureau. Usually enumerators don't talk to homeowners, unless there's a discrepancy between the HHC list and what's "on the ground," as we say in the Bureau. But I've heard that sometimes enumerators do talk to residents. Like when they're being chased off a property with a gun, or like one enumerator who went to a home, knocked, and was greeted by a naked man—a man whom the enumerator recognized from church. The interview was conducted without a word about, well, you know.

Now, I say that "I've heard that enumerators talk to residents" because I never actually went to any housing units. I worked a total of 40 hours for the Census. Less, if you don't count our hour-long lunches, the two 20-minute breaks each day, the morning we were locked out of the training room, or the day we got out at 1 p.m. because it was 70 degrees and sunny. When I say "worked," I mean I went through the training. And when I say "training," I mean I spent most of the time filling out withholding forms, confidentiality forms, payroll forms, form forms, etc. I was even "sworn in" as a government worker after 15 minutes. When our trainer told us to stand and take an oath, I looked around to see if he was joking. And then I was put in charge of the HHCs while everyone went on a 20-minute break.

Anyway, I went home after training and waited to be assigned work. The following Thursday I got the call: "Hello, this is Phyllis from the Census."

"Great," I replied.

"I need to pick up your official Census Bureau badge and official Census Bureau messenger bag. There's no work. I don't know why they trained you guys; they knew the work was done in your area."

I met her at Brown's County Market to return my gear. I was hoping for a black sedan and dark sunglasses; I got Phyllis in a Dodge minivan and Cubs jacket. My glamorous career in the Bureau was over.

Now, I don't write this as another study on government inefficiency. I think the census is important because it helps communities figure out how to use tax dollars and what services are needed for a changing population. And I don't write this 'cause I'm angry about the job. I didn't expect much anyway. I write this because I liked the people I trained with. It was only 40 hours, but everyone there was in the same boat; everyone needed to make extra money. Just so you know, there was a downturn in the economy in 2008. Yeah, sorry to break it to you. So there were white collar folks, some realtors, a school board member, a community activist. Some 20-somethings, some realtors, a single mom, a widower, some retirees. And some realtors. All had a good sense of humor. Most had a distrust of government (the oath should've included: "We acknowledge that we are now officially part of the problem").

Everyone was just trying to make ends meet. I was looking for supplemental work because I direct a not-for-profit, and the freelance writing I did on the side had dried up. But I have nothing to complain about. I had lunch with one of my fellow trainees who'd been out of work for over a year. He couldn't find a truck driving job to save his life. And three months before our training, his wife passed away. His house was in foreclosure because her income was gone, and he ended up having to move into his brother's house. But you know what he said? "The Lord has provided every step of the way. Yessir. Yessir." Pray for that guy.

I'm grateful for my career in the Bureau, however short-lived. I met some people who are persevering in situations more difficult than mine—people who are exhibiting resiliency and gratitude. There should be a movie about that.

Quotidian Meeting of Insomnia Committee

Quotidian Meeting of Insomnia Committee
Date: March 23, 2014; 2 a.m.

Location: Best Western, Nashville, TN; Room 203.

Attendance: Myself.

Approval of March 22 Meeting Minutes: The committee met yesterday, March 22, 2 a.m. Discussion was tabled at 5 a.m. until the March 23 meeting. Committee will most likely meet despite being on vacation. Minutes approved.

Agenda:
Old Business: Denial of meeting. Review of upcoming monumental decisions, through 2018. Regrets: 1967 to Present. Metaphysical ponderings. Prayers for slumber mercies.

New Business: Roundtable Discussion: Q: "Why did you find it necessary to have that ice cream after all that fried chicken at Hattie B's? I mean, really? Come on." Discussion tabled. Roundtable Discussion: Q: "Why are you being so irritable around your daughter lately? Is it really because she doesn't empty the dishwasher? Or is it because she'll be heading off to college in the fall? Both?" Discussion tabled. Roundtable Discussion: Q: "What time does the complimentary breakfast begin in the lobby? 6 o'clock?"

Motion to adjourn meeting passed at 5:56 a.m.

Next Meeting: March 24, 2 a.m. Best Western, Nashville, TN; Room 203.

Respectfully submitted.

Bloom Son

Everything is blooming around here. If you're quiet, you might be able to hear it; it grows so fast, overnight, in this weather. My farmer friend, Mark, says he can hear the corn when it grows.

My middle school son is almost as tall as me after this winter, which is no great feat, but still. And his voice is changing. I kept one of this boy's voice messages, from just a year ago, on my phone. I've listened to it a few times this week. You can hear him grow.

Beautiful

There is this retired woman in my church. And I work with middle school students in our church. This woman's only son is in his thirties and has kids of his own. Yet she called me last year to see if she could provide snacks for the middle school group. I said, "Of course! Thank you so much!"

Middle school students are to snacks as coyotes are to Yorkshire Terriers. There is circling, growling, snapping, and tearing. Bits and pieces flying everywhere in the frenzy. And then, "Can we please, please, please have another Yorkshire Terrier? No?"

More growling. Of course I am exaggerating. About the coyotes.

So, when this woman said she would provide snacks, I imagined generic packages of duplex creme cookies, à la Vacation Bible School: hard, bland, dry. Perfect for middle school students who are more about quantity of food than quality of food.

She said she would bring them on the first Wednesday of each month. And she did:

June: Your choice of gourmet, home-baked cookies: Vermont Maple Pecan; Apple Spice; Vermont Maple (w/o nuts).

July: Homemade cinnamon rolls with sumptuous, coffee flavored icing.

August: Giant, decadent, chocolate chip brownies served with peppermint stick ice cream.

September: Warm, jumbo, soft pretzels with your choice of dipping sauces: honey mustard, spicy mustard, and jalapeno mustard.

October: Pumpkin spice bars crowned with rich cream cheese frosting.

November: Warm apple pie squares coupled with vanilla ice cream

And on and on. Never the same thing twice. The kids can hardly believe it. They now anticipate, via coyote instincts, the first Wednesday of each month, and they run and salivate all the way to the church kitchen.

I never see her deliver these gourmet masterpieces. They just appear. The students don't know this woman. They couldn't pick her out of a congregational line-up. And she doesn't know their names either. She just decided to give. Not only to give, but to lavish upon these kids her time, resources, and gifts. She goes above and beyond the letter of the law of "Bring Snacks." Above and beyond the letter of the law of "Love Your Neighbor." Many times I read Jesus' command as "Don't harm your neighbor." Or, "Wave to your neighbor." Or, "Be nice to your neighbor." But this woman hears it as "Initiate lavish hospitality with strangers," and "Extravagantly bless a bunch of middle schoolers."

On the first Wednesday of each month we learn much more about the love of God from this woman than from anything I am teaching. I won't tell you this woman's name. She'd be embarrassed. But I will give you a clue: Her name is derived from the Scottish word for "beautiful." No surprise.

Sweet Corn

This is the summer of plowing the crops under. A time of drought and brush fires.

It's the year of dead limbs and diseased trees. A season of dry grass that never sees the mower.

But today, on the west edge of town, down by the grain elevator: sweet corn. A blue pick-up from out of town piled high with fat green and gold ears. From some storehouse of hope two counties over.

And at my grandma's cottage on Lake Sherwood in July, we used to eat that corn on the cob and pretend we were typewriters. *Tap. Tap. Tap. Ding. Return. Slide.* Journalists with salt and butter hands reporting that the forecast calls for rain.

Job's Wisconsin
(The Book of Job, chapters 38–41; a paraphrase)

Tell me, who is it that churns up the mighty Wolf River like a cheap washing machine for you at Big Smokey Falls?

Have you ever rounded up herds of mosquitoes and sent them on their summer stampede?

Do you know why the ferocious, but slow, snapping turtle springs his jaws like a trap and won't let go?

Who can call up Aurora Borealis for a command performance above Nicolet, as you lie on your back in the long, wet grass? She dances through several wardrobe changes, and there you are slack-jawed and prostrate.

Can you pour humidity through a sieve upon old women and play havoc with their permanents?

Or send forth the sun's heat so fierce that white central-Wisconsin thighs stick to black vinyl car seats?

Can you pull in a trout with a fishhook, or put him in a net? Or, are you only privy to where the bluegill lives? Have you ever caught a fish big enough to eat, or fried one in a pan, under the moon at Devil's Lake?

Do you know why all the traffic gets dammed up on I-90 just south of Madison, precisely when your bladder is about to rupture? And then begins to flow again as if nothing happened? Tell me if you do.

And who endowed the bald eagle with eyes that can see for a mile? Even around that bend in the Wolf River, to see if we're still together?

Circus World Museum

The small town of Baraboo, Wisconsin, is home to the Circus World Museum. Fifty acres of circus history in the town that the Ringling Brothers used as their winter quarters from 1884 to 1918.

I remember my grandparents taking us to this circus cathedral when we were little. Actually, my grandma would take us. My grandpa was simply the chauffeur. Cloistered in his air-conditioned Oldsmobile, under the gaze of sorrowful Dashboard St. Mary, my grandfather would contemplate the *Milwaukee Sentinel*, dial in the Brewers game, and wait for us to return.

As we entered the museum, there was a giant gorilla in a circus train car cage. Terrifying and fake. But what if, well, he suddenly wasn't fake? It could happen. Next was the trumpeting, wheezing calliope. (One time, I remember a reporter on Channel 5 doing a feature on the calliopes of Circus World Museum. He pronounced it "CAL-ee-ope," like it rhymed with antelope, through the entire segment.) That monster ape and gasping, pipe organ cacophony ushered us into the museum. I remember being excited for, and afraid of, what I would see. I loved it.

Not long ago, in July, my wife and kids and I visited this historical site on the way to go camping at Devil's Lake. Twenty-five years after my last visit, probably. And it is beautiful; my kids loved it.

In one building at the Circus World Museum, there are cracked black-and-white photos of faithful elephants. In another display, there is a scratchy, hollow recording of a ringmaster calling the Big Top into glorious action. And, over there, in a glass case, are faded garments covered in dull sequins, once worn by the Flying Wallendas and other high-wire risk takers walking by faith. Next to them, a case full of clown props used to show up human absurdity. And just up the hill from there are housed hundreds of majestic, filigreed circus wagons, once used to carry this show to cities around the nation.

Then there is that red and white sideshow tent outside, where there are wax figures of menacing giants, fearless snake handlers, a tattooed woman whose skin tells a mysterious story, and Siamese twins who are connected one to another with a bond I could never understand.

Twice a day, there is a Big Top show on the hot, dusty grounds, with some very tired looking clowns and a sleepy organ player, where the most active member of the event is the attendant with the shovel who runs along behind the elephants.

All this to say—and upon further reflection—I'm not sure there should be a circus museum. Something rings hollow. It's all very interesting and beautiful, but where is the thunder? Where is the clatter of hooves and wheels taking this show on the road? Where is the glory of this strange spectacle, the likes of which the world has never seen? Is this where children are supposed to run away to?

The very essence of the circus is movement. Don't fence it in and flatten it out. It's about bringing risk, danger, excitement, and wildness right to peoples' front doors. To reduce it to permanent displays, models, and reminiscence that require us to come to it is, at best, looking through the wrong end of the telescope. At worst, it is a denial of the circus' reality. No offense intended toward the Wisconsin State Historical Society, but I suggest they free those elephants from the leg shackles of "used-to-be" and "remember-when." We need them now more than ever.

Maybe that's why my grandpa wouldn't come in, but sat in the car with Mother Mary and Paul Molitor. Maybe my grandfather was afraid of what he wouldn't see.

Of course, I am not talking about the Circus World Museum.

Firework

My mother called me. Then my brother called and said, "It's his independence day."

Grandpa Halverson passed away on July 4th in Port Edwards, Wisconsin. He was 93. I'd meant to call him that week.

I was at a fireworks display with friends when I got the news. Grandpa was worth crying over right then and there. And soon the fireworks started. Whistles and green rockets bursting into pinwheels. Thunder and white blooms crackling and plummeting to earth. Booms and red corkscrews in whirling dervish. An overwhelming display.

In between all of that—in those split seconds of darkness—are the ghosts. Those almost undetectable columns and wisps of gray-white smoke against black sky. One for each firework. They float off with the wind, exiting stage left. A slow drift parade. A flickering silent film.

And then on to the next flash and bang.

Underneath all of this, in the band shell, the municipal band is conjuring up a frenzied set of show tunes, marches, and patriotic numbers, unable to see the display going on right above their heads. They miss it all, year after year.

Life is too much. Too fast. I miss a great deal of it. Someday, I intend to run for city council on the platform that we change the annual fireworks display to the annual firework display. After we all take our seats on blankets and lawn chairs, there will be one firework. We can marvel at its light, and its color, and its sound, and its smell, and its shape against the darkness. And at its pall as it passes. Then we will move our mouths in awe and shake our heads in astonishment: *Will you look at that? Good Lord, can you believe it?*

We will wonder about such beauty: *How was it made? Who can take it all in?* Then we will go home, trembling in silence. It will be worth crying over right then and there.

Fish Skin Confession

I am on the dock.

I am holding this red-eyed, smallmouth bass, with the thick dark skin. Holding it by the line. She is hooked for good. My daughter has caught her, when all the boy cousins have failed dozens of times this vacation to catch the stoic, immovable fish. My family—wife, kids, sister, sister-in-law, nephews, mother— all standing on the dock with me. But the cheers for *Catch!* have now turned to protests of *Release!* Be careful what you wish for.

I am stuck holding the bass. Caught on a line. The place I am most afraid to be. I have never handled a fish this big. I can do bluegills. Crappie. Sunfish. Pumpkinseed. Sliding my whole hand over slippery scales, to press down sharp spines. Feeling the up-and-down breathing, now pulling the hook to release the fish. Granting mercy. Tossing them back. But I'm nervous around this much wildness. That's part of it: Nervous around teeth and spines. More, I am afraid of public humiliation, of people discovering that I have no idea what I'm doing. That I am not a man, but a boy. I've never done this before. I'm 44 years old and I'm afraid. Hemingway would not have written *The Man Who Was Afraid of a Fish*.

I am on the dock. I am in the dock.

"Should I call your brother to get it off the hook?" my mom worries behind me. My brother is up in the cabin. "Yes, please," the bass says. "Let's get someone in here who knows how to release."

"Come on, mom! Geez!" I cast an angry glance at her for calling me into question. Fish working against the hook, and the line in my hand.

"You come on!" she flares, surprising herself. She is a rescuer by nature: mentally disturbed dogs and needy people, now smallmouth bass, apparently. Compassionate to a fault.

I want to simply cut the line and let the fish drop into the water with the jig still hooked in its mouth. Its skin will just grow over it, right? I've heard of that, or seen people catch fish with hooks incorporated into their flesh. An inconvenience—something you deal with as a fish. It is what it is; it's just fish life. But I'm not equipped; my jackknife is in the cabin, too. One has to hook fingers under the fish jaw, I know. I've seen it on television. Under this thin skin place, through the flesh.

How can it have a built-in, open wound like this? My fingers slip in, doubting how this will all end. I can feel the smallmouth bass' jaws, like sandstone, rubbing together. Grinding in worry, impatience. Sandstone, sandpaper.

"I cannot swing here all day, suffocating, waiting for you to decide what you're gonna do," the bass says.

So I work at pulling the hook, like a civil war dentist. The patient languishing.

But, finally, it comes free. Yes! God, yes. Who can believe it? My fingers slipping out of the bass, letting her fall back into the lake. Ker-plunk. Finally, some redemption. I did it.

But she's on her side. Red eye to the heavens. I waited too long. The family stands along the edge of the dock, casting their eyes downward. The sun, prickly hot on my skin.

Thin skin. Open wound. Thin places. I think that's what Celtic believers called them. Places where one feels closest to God, where heaven and earth come together. Places to touch and be touched by God. Like those places on Lake Michigan where I go to sit and be quiet. But I don't believe the "thin places" are always pleasant. Sometimes God sticks his finger in our wound. Feels around to see if we're for real. "Oh Thomas, what does your open wound—that vulnerable spot—have to say about you?"

I look down to the floating bass and feel the finger of God. Exposed here in the dock, I confess I do not have it all together, like I pretend. This simple act of removing a fish from a hook—an act performed by five-year-olds—has exposed my pride and my fears. What in real-time was 60 seconds, felt like an hour.

This is a thin place. But, struggling with a fish hook is not the charge. "Where are you? What are you hiding?" God asks. The charge I bring against myself is fraud. I am afraid that others will see that I am afraid.

"Look," my daughter exclaims, interrupting the wake for the bass around the dock.

A ripple, and the bass thrusts her tail downward. Once more, down. And again, down. Reclaiming her watch on the sandy bottom.

Off the hook. Out of the dock.

We cheer again, for mercy's sake. For new life. And no one says a word about it afterward. Amen.

El Gaucho

Dear Man,

I strongly recommend that you grow a mustache if you have not already done so. By no means am I an expert, but when I have grown a mustache in the past the results have been spectacular. I am not bragging.

Primarily, you should grow a mustache because you can, but there are other benefits as well. You should grow a mustache because it gets things done. Yes, you will face opposition from your wife: "Okay, are we about done with the roustabout look?" Friends who are really no more than acquaintances will say: "Dude, you look like a truck driver." Your teenage daughter will take it as one more opportunity for ridicule: "Who's that creeper in our summer vacation photos? Oh, that's Dad." Yes, initially your mustache may look like coffee grounds glued to a Smokey the Bear preschool project. But nothing worth having comes easy. Or looks very good to begin with. Or starts without feeling itchy. This is the fourth law of physics, and its corollaries.

So tell your wife, and the other naysayers, this: Two summers ago my family and I were on vacation in Wisconsin. Our Subaru with Illinois plates broke down, so I called a local mechanic for a tow and repair. This is a recipe for disaster. Did I mention I was in Wisconsin with a broken down Subaru with Illinois plates? I might as well have put a sign on my back that read: "Crack me in the head with your monkey wrench and take my wallet. Please."

Luckily, earlier in the summer, I had grown a mustache. My best mustache ever. I fondly referred to it as "El Gaucho." I have heard it referred to regionally as "The Biker," "The Warrior," and "The Pancho Villa." Sometimes, mistakenly, "The Fu Manchu." My wife referred to it as "that thing." For two months, "El Gaucho" presided over my top lip and trailed commandingly down the sides of my face to the brink of each jowl. Even now I miss it. Him.

Anyway, the mechanic—who also had a mustache—came to tow the car, and we talked and joked for an extraordinary amount of time. Previously I would have trembled with suspicion in the presence of an auto mechanic. Later, I would realize that it was my mustache that was doing the talking. The mustache was going before me, greasing the wheel. Now greasing the palm. Because, not more than three hours later, I received a call that the car was done. Three hours. The cost? Ninety dollars. Can you believe it? Under "Illinois Tourist Car Repair" on Wisconsin mechanics' service menus, the usual price is $500 to $1,000.

Thank you, El Gaucho.

Tell your wife that. And tell her how on that entire vacation we got tables more quickly at restaurants. We received better service. And I believe we received discounts where before there had been none. Mustaches get things done. Sadly, at the end of the summer, I succumbed to familial pressure to remove it. El Emasculacion, in Spanish.

It wasn't until this fall that I resurrected "El Gaucho." So as not to arouse suspicion, I started with a beard, but soon after carved away the superfluous to reveal my Old Friend. The responses were the same from my family. Blah, blah, blah.

But one Tuesday night, mustache in tow, I was working at a reading program at an income-eligible apartment complex in our community. We provide reading and homework help for kids. A preschool girl named Hailey and I were engrossed in putting together a circus animal puzzle on the floor. With no announcement, she stood and stuck her hand in my face. Hailey rubbed it back and forth across my mustache for about five seconds. One monkey. Two monkey. Three monkey. Four monkey. Five monkey. That's a long time. Then she whispered to her friend, "Mia, come see this."

And Mia did.

Then Hailey patted me on the head like a dog. It was funny. But later I thought maybe it wasn't so funny. In most low-income apartment complexes there are very few men. Almost every family is a single mom and kids. And from what I had heard, Hailey's dad, or step-dad, was in prison. So a mustache, and a man for that matter, must have been a strange animal. It reinforced for me that a mustache gets things done, whether it be reduced auto repair bills or, more importantly, building bridges with kids who need some healthy male influence and connection. This particular mustache grabbing incident reminded me that men have some responsibility to act like a dad to kids who need one.

So in conclusion, Man, you should grow a mustache. Because you can. And the cost of that ability is responsibility. Winston Churchill said something like that. Just think how much more he could have accomplished had he sported a powerful "El Gaucho."

Godspeed in your efforts.

Warm Regards.

Significant

My wedding ring is sitting somewhere at the bottom of Sugar Creek, near Crawfordsville, Indiana. I was shocked when I realized it was gone. I showed my wife my bare ring finger.

"For real?"

"Yeah. I don't even know when it happened. It's just gone."

She nodded and smiled. "It's okay, we're still married. I still love you."

I was surprised and glad that she took it so easily. But I felt sad, and a bit lost. Disappointed. It isn't even a good story. I didn't have to cut it off because I was pinned under rocks in a canyon. I didn't have to destroy it in a volcano in order to break the powers of darkness that enslaved the world. No. I just went tubing and canoeing with friends through that shallow river on a July day. And it was gone.

I am no fan of Indiana, so it feels like an even bigger waste. Don't even get me started on Indiana.

But then she asked, "Do you think it means anything?"

"Well," I said, "I think it means my ring slipped off in a river. I don't think it's a sign."

But the ring *is* a sign. Significant. More than I thought. I see now how often I push my thumb up my palm, and against the ring, to rotate it, clockwise. While I'm thinking, or when I'm nervous. But now my thumb doesn't find the ring. It had been on my finger for over 23 years.

If you find it in the river, it means you're in Indiana, and I feel sorry for you. You'll know it's mine by its inside inscription: "I love you Matt."

Yeah.

Since the day she put it on me, it's always been the joke: "Who's Matt? Is this from a pawn shop? Am I a back-up?"

It actually says, "I love you Matt 19:6." The jeweler just had trouble squeezing it all in. Matt 19:6 is a reference to the Gospel of Matthew. Chapter 19, and verse six. Jesus' words about marriage: "So they are no longer two but one flesh. What therefore God has joined together, let not man separate."

So, the ring is a sign of divine arithmetic: one plus one is one. A sign of the divine tether that ties us together. A reminder that, as far as earthly things go, I'm not going to find anything more tightly woven. I feel sorry for Matt, wherever he may be, that he missed out on this—untethered, wandering the wasteland of Indiana maybe. Pray for Matt, if you think of him.

And when I pulled my left hand up out of Sugar Creek and noticed my loss, I also noticed a scar. Half-inch, pale, raised, a quarter inch above, and parallel to, the knuckle. It's always covered by the ring, so I forget about it. It's from helping Dave Lewis solder two copper pipes together in his basement 20 years ago. I held them tight, while he used the blow torch. The solder turned to silver liquid, dripped off the pipe and onto my skin, and burned me beneath my ring. It seared a divot into my flesh. I remember not wanting to let go so that Dave's pipes would stick together. I always remember my friend Dave when I remove my ring. But now that the ring is gone, I see the scar all the time.

The ring serves to cover divots and old wounds. It is significant because it covers my shortcomings. And my brokenness. My wife is the better person, between the two of us. Everybody knows it. She is smarter. She is more wise. She is more thoughtful. If I go to the grocery store for bread, milk, and butter, I will return with the bread and milk. If she goes to the grocery store for bread, milk, and butter, she returns with the bread, milk, and butter, and a snack for our son's lunch because she knows he has a golf tournament tomorrow and that he'll be hungry on the bus ride after school. But, on the other side, my wife might say that I am wise, too, and that I help her slow down, and make her laugh, and remind her of the big picture when she is in tears over details.

No one knows the extent of our insecurities and failures, except the other. The ring encircles those secrets, and creates safe places to be vulnerable and reveal old wounds. If I told you everything about me, you might be surprised and disappointed. She knows everything and still has not left. Not once in over 23 years.

I lost my ring in that river over two months ago. My wife keeps asking, "When are we going shopping? I think you're getting too used to being without it." And it's true, I am dragging my feet when it comes to getting a new one. Because how do you replace something that was imbued with so much significance, and emotion, and hope on that hot day back in May of 1991? Getting a new one would feel like trading Wisconsin for Indiana, maybe. And I so dislike Indiana. But I need to get over that and pick a new sign. The old one was significant, but still only a sign of the real deal.

And that's something we will not lose by accident in some river in Indiana.

Funeral for Summer

It's hard to believe she's gone. But I'm sure I speak for everyone here when I say our lives are better—richer—because she was around.

We've laid her out in yellows, and oranges, and reds. I think that's what she would have wanted. Let everyone take one last long look.

When Summer was here, do you remember how we would spend all day on the beach in Egg Harbor, after breakfast at the Village Café? Digging holes and making monuments with the white rocks, trying to hold back the waters of Green Bay. And afterward, the kids buried each other in that sand. We reclined in the cool water and shuddered upon slipping in for the first time. Some kind of group baptism into a new life of rest.

"We pronounce you dead to frantic busyness . . ."

Dunk!

Gasp!

"But raised to new life," the gulls squawked. Or at least raised to a few moments of sticking our heads above water and breathing deep. In the name of the Father, and of the Son, and of the Holy Ghost, I threw my keys, and my watch, and my calendar in a drawer and lost track of them for that week in Door County. Amen.

It seems like only yesterday, but when Summer was here, we all sat on that screened-in porch every night after dinner. The stars spilled out across the inky darkness. The moon rose again over the bluff. The Green Bay breezes awakened the beach towels and swimsuits on the makeshift clothesline. The perfect time to try Le Faux Grain de Raisin—another bad bottle of red wine we'd never heard of. And outside in the yellow porch light glow, under the pines, niece and nephews performed an impromptu talent show. A hip-hop theatre of the absurd. Each act disintegrated into elementary kids snorting and falling down. Cirque Duh So Lame.

Then that kamikaze bat dive-bombed the stage. Screams! The curtain fell and the kids tumbled onto the porch for their reviews:

"Great choreography, but lacked passion," my brother said.

"Creative, but needed a stronger finish," their grandmother said.

"I don't get it," my sister said.

But, in the end, "Poignant. Riveting. Delightfully lowbrow," *The Chronicle* reported.

Because of Summer, and because of that porch, I remembered how much I like all of you. And wondered why we see each other so little the rest of the year. Life is so short.

Today, we commit Summer to the leaf pile and a good Autumn wind. Ashes to ashes, and dust to dust. But there is no need for tears, because we have the hope of resurrection. That as surely as Winter is coming, Spring will follow. And then Summer, again.

Don't be discouraged.

Was it Pascal who said, "What is harder to believe, that something that was alive at one time could come alive again? Or, that something that never was could be in the first place?" Yes. Something like that. Now is the time to practice hope, brothers and sisters. God rest our beautiful Summer. Amen. And, amen.

Please join us for a coffee and egg salad sandwich luncheon after the service. In lieu of flowers, gifts of beach towels and Le Faux Grain de Raisin can be left on the front porch. Go in peace.

This Is Practice

My son gave me a haircut today.

It is my first haircut since the COVID-19 shutdown started. We are four weeks into stay-at-home orders for the pandemic.

I don't make appointments for haircuts. My hair just reaches a length where I can no longer stand it and I am propelled to the barber shop. I've even left work to get a haircut. But, during the quarantine, barber shops are some of the businesses categorized as "non-essential," and are closed. Some essential businesses are pet salons, McDonald's, and liquor stores, I guess. Anyway, when I can't just run out to get my fix when I feel overwhelmed with this pile of hair, I get a bit obsessive: "I need a haircut"; "This is driving me crazy"; "Do you see this? I gotta get this cut." There is a lot of hair on this head; I get it from my mom's side. My grandpa had big hair 'til the day he died at 93.

The idea that barber shops and salons are non-essential is a mis-categorization, in my opinion. When I am getting a non-pandemic haircut, and I look around the establishment, I think it is more a holy ministry than a service transaction. The stylists are the Sisters of Perpetual Relief and Neck Trims, offering hospitality, one-on-one human contact, conversation, human touch, close care, and "You look good!"

I seem to remember my grandma going weekly to her hairdresser. She'd emerge later, hair in a headscarf to keep it from blowing about. I know other seniors, too, who do the same thing. Does one need her "hair done" every week? No. But does it contribute to her dignity and sense of community? Yes.

In the end, though, it's care we must pay for.

I ask my son, who is 20, and home early from college for distance learning, to give me a trim. He happily agrees. We head to the bathroom and choose the number two clipper guard. He places his hand on my shoulder. He glides the clippers around the sides and back of my head. "Oops!" he jokes. There is some vulnerability as he stands behind me and wields those blades at my neck, but I am reminded that this is an act of care. We are father and son. We are friends. I sift the brown and gray clumps of hair through my fingers as they drop into the bathroom sink. It's an even mix of colors now, but one day, sooner rather than later, the gray will prevail and my son may have to care for me more than this. I need to learn to be vulnerable and reliant—to move away from "I can do this alone" to "I could use your help." This is good for both of us in a small way.

A week later, I am in the bathroom with *my* father. He has fallen at his house in Wisconsin. I am there to-drive him to his heart surgery at the Mayo Clinic. His surgery will be to repair the heart valve he had replaced 18 years ago. It has begun leaking and causes him exhaustion, shortness of breath, weakness, and imbalance. Thus he is lying on the floor. Thus, he is too weak to pull himself up. We struggle together, me behind him, trying to pull him up. Now dragging him to his bedside so we can pull him up to sitting. We struggle together for 30 minutes but we finally get him upright. He pants, "This is embarrassing."

I can't even imagine.

The last time he fell, during the holidays, it was in his kitchen and I caught him against my shoulder when his ankles gave way. Leaning heavily on me, under his breath, he cursed in my ear, "Dammit." He cursed like someone being chased, whose pursuer had caught up with him. We are all being chased.

Back in **my** bathroom, my son clicks off the clippers, looks in the mirror with me, and reassures, "That doesn't look bad, does it?" And it doesn't. He does a good job for me. I'm thankful. I offer to cut his hair, but he declines for the time being—maybe he's not as confident with me at the clippers.

How will we emerge from this health crisis? I don't know. Mangey haircuts? Misshapen heads? Maybe, but perhaps we will have been cared for by each other, because we needed help. And my haircut doesn't look bad, does it? It's not the point, anyway. During this pandemic we are reminded that life is uncertain, and that we are not in control. Sooner rather than later, we will all find ourselves needing help in the mirror or on the bathroom floor. Or elsewhere. I need to practice needing help now. To practice asking for help. It will be good for everyone.

I'll Never Go Back to that Library

In the winter I was chatting with a friend about books. She's 80. She loves Westerns. Loves John Wayne. I told her about a book she should check out from the library.

"Nope," she replied. "One time I checked out a book about John Wayne. It made him look bad. I'll never go back to that library again."

I laughed, but she was serious. And then I was sad, thinking of all the stories she's missing out on by wanting to hear that one, one-sided story over and over.

But here we all are a few months later, in the COVID-19 pandemic. We have never experienced anything like this with all the lockdowns, the cancellations, the uncertainty. And here I am, rewatching old movies, rereading old books. Revisiting old recipes. Listening to old Innocence Mission albums on vinyl, every day for weeks. It's all comfort and known quantities. I know how they all end, and the world makes sense again.

Soon I will want to hear new stories—and tell new stories—but for now I get it, Friend.

Look at This, Neighbor

"Culture is not a territory to be won or lost but a resource we are called to steward with care. Culture is a garden to be cultivated." –Makoto Fujimura

There was a protest two nights ago at the courthouse in our small town. The protest was over the George Floyd killing in Minneapolis. If this has reached as far as our little Midwest community, then there is a foundation being shaken in our country.

My family went because it's our town, and because we want to love our neighbor—but don't know how. We went to listen to and see our neighbor. I assumed we'd hear a few speeches on the courthouse steps over a P.A., then head home after an hour. That's neat and tidy.

We were surprised that maybe 400 people had gathered. More surprised that the protest began with kneeling in silence for nine minutes—about the amount of time the police officer knelt on Floyd's neck—and all the communal discomfort, reflection, tears even, and prayer that go with it.

We all knelt. Black, brown, white. Very old, very young. The mayor, police officers, educators, business owners. This was church. After the nine minutes, which felt like a lifetime, the high school student leaders said, over a bullhorn, ""Now we're going to march, that way."

Marching? I was wearing flip flops. I wasn't prepared for the endurance required for this protest. We walked west through downtown, then south, east, and north, past bars, restaurants, banks, and churches, all just reopening after months of lockdown due to COVID-19. We walked some of the same route as our annual Pumpkin Festival parade.

Call and response shouting: "Black lives matter!"; "No justice, no peace!" or "No peace, no justice." I'm not sure.

And, "Hands up! Don't shoot!" I couldn't say that one. It didn't feel like mine to say. I was an observer-participant, but it felt like repentance to be there.

Walking next to me was a maybe-eight-year-old white girl with her family, and she had this look of shock and confusion the whole time, like, "What is happening here? Something is wrong, and I don't understand it. The world is different than I thought."

I'm putting that on her, of course, but her face reflected what I was experiencing. The evening was church: beautiful and sorrowful, revelatory and visceral. Peaceful but agitating. Stewardship and cultivation. Not "Us vs. Them," but more "Look at This, Neighbor. Say His Name. Say Her Name."

To Whom It May Concern

To Whom It May Concern,

I am writing to recommend Autumn for the position recently left vacant by Summer. I have observed Autumn's work for the last 40 years or so, and feel I am as qualified as anyone to comment on her abilities.

For at least the past 40 years, Autumn has faithfully and without complaint ushered in Packer football seasons, kicked off school years, and provided meaningful work for sweater manufacturers and kids with rakes. She has been a major sponsor of the annual harvest of pumpkins, apples, cauliflower, brussels sprouts, and zucchini, to name a few. I don't even have to mention how each year she hosts that beloved children's event: Halloween. And, of course, her crowning achievement: the fall color display in collaboration with the trees of our community. Her management skills have allowed all of these to come off like clockwork.

Of course, it would be difficult in this space to elaborate on all of her accomplishments. I understand that in the eyes of a few, Summer has left some big shoes to fill. However, sometimes big shoes just mean they were on the clearance rack. As you consider Autumn for this position, let me be candid: this has not been a stellar year for Summer. Yes, there was that sunny week in June, the fireworks were okay, and the spinach came up nicely. But personally, I think any loudmouth with an associate's degree in P.E. could do what Summer does. This year, I am sure many would agree, she phoned it in. Like the waiter at that lakeside bar and grill, who seemed so friendly and funny at first: "How's it goin', Boss? What can I do you for?" Ha. Ha. Ha. But he was nowhere to be found when it came to refilling your Diet RC Cola, or bringing that bottle of A.1. Steak Sauce after you'd asked for it three times. If he thought he was going to escape without eating one of my signature piercing glares in tip reduction sauce, he was deluded. Anyway, if you check the time cards, Summer showed up late for the first day of work. About three weeks late, as I recall. And there were days, even weeks on end, where she was absent without as much as a phone call. For example, my one week of vacation: 63 degrees and rainy. Come on! This is July 30, people! Any chimp with *The Old*

Farmer's Almanac could have done a better job. But enough about Summer's lack of aptitude, I am writing on behalf of Autumn.

I understand this is just seasonal work, but Autumn's abilities cannot be overstated, and she would be perfect to pick up where Summer left off. In fact, she would bring a necessary change of direction. After the mindless, devil-may-care stupor that Summer left us with, you'll find that Autumn will create a much-needed atmosphere of introspection: How did we do this year? What will we do with the time we have left? To whom can we give all this zucchini?

I highly recommend Autumn to you for this opportunity. She is clearly the next logical step for your organization. Thank you for your consideration.

Kind Regards.

7:40 A.M., Sabin Street: An Observation

Bleary-eyed moms, outside at the bus stop, wave farewell to their kindergartners who climb aboard the school bus. All the mothers wave with both hands. Like people do when they are drowning. More, they wave with both hands like people do when they're about to be rescued from drowning. Hallelujah! Thank you, Jesus.

Deer Call

Coconut & Peppermint. Soap Bark & Chamomile. Honey & Bilberry.

All in my house at this moment in one form or another: sprays, fresheners, hand soaps. That's all there are now. Sophisticated, gourmet fragrances. Atmosphere-creating scents. I have no idea what bilberry is. Or soap bark. I think we're just making things up now.

Growing up, besides Lysol, the only scent we had was "pine." No, not White Spruce & Cranberries, just "pine." Green pine, if you need an adjective, and not like any pine I had ever smelled in the woods. Pretty sure it was a joke from the factory. But there was no pretense. It was just "pine."

Mahogany & Teakwood doesn't transport me anywhere, but that pine scent takes me places. To Wisconsin Rapids, Wisconsin. To the backseat of my grandfather's Olds 88. Air-conditioning set to "arctic." Radio set to easy-listening: "You're tuned to Beautiful Music Stereo." The pine tree freshener spinning under the rearview mirror, and above dashboard Mother Mary.

The pine takes me further to this memory: Elementary school. My grandparents, and my sister and I, were returning from Herschleb's Ice Cream. These trips were always filled with suspense, as my grandfather would purposely mispronounce the names when he ordered: maple nut was MOP-lee NUT; chocolate was chuh-CALL-it.

On this particular trip, on the way back to my grandparents' house at dusk, we spotted a dozen deer in a field off of 48th Street South. My grandfather pulled the car over to the shoulder and told us, "I'm going to use my deer call."

He got out of the car, walked to the front, cupped his hands over his mouth, and let out a loud, warbling, turkey-like ululation. And then he did it again.

The deer did not come, but neither did they run away. They perked up with heads cocked, ears twitching, and stared at my grandfather: "What the devil?" The same looks we gave from the backseat. Then, my grandfather got back in the car.

"Huh, usually they come," he said.

And we drove off without explanation. It took a minute, and a few side glances, 'til we were pretty sure it was a joke. "What just happened here?" Then, we laughed. And I have been laughing at this for over 40 years since, whenever I think of it. I'm still pretty sure it was a joke. This unsophisticated, goofball, dramatically comedic act took place in the atmosphere of that chilled, wafting pine scent. My grandfather did not take himself so seriously that he would miss an opportunity to entertain a small, captive audience of children.

My guess is this would not happen under the auspices of Cucumber & Melon. Or Mango & Hibiscus. Or White Tea & Ginger.

Smoke Beard

"Your beard smells like campfire."

My wife said that to me after I returned from a few days of camping at Devil's Lake in Wisconsin. At the moment she said it, I realized it was the only thing I've ever longed to hear from anyone. I didn't know it beforehand, but I know it now: this was what I was waiting to hear my whole life.

Here are the reasons why, in no particular order (except that I've numbered them): First, it means that I have a beard, which is reason enough. Yes, beards are a trendy, pop culture thing right now, like bacon is a trendy, pop culture thing right now. I am too old to be trendy, and the trend doesn't devalue either beards or bacon. The value in having a beard is the same value in, say, having one's own garden. Something homegrown, manageable, and fruitful in this whelming world. What's the harvest, you ask? Think bonsai, rather than pumpkin patch, friend. Yes, a beard is a bonsai for the face. A trim of the creeping mustache, a snip of a stray whisker, a pluck of that aesthetically offending nose hair. Facial hair is its own reward. A contemplative stroke of one's beard is the fruit of one's labor. Plus, everyone wants a beard. Everyone. Don't lie.

The second reason that "Your-beard-smells-like-campfire" resonates so deeply is that it means I have been somewhere. Wood smoke, bug spray, and coffee, I believe, are the best fragrances on this earth. Limes down the garbage disposal and cheap gin round out the top five. But those first three scents suggest that I had exchanged the glow of my computer screen for the flicker of a campfire for a time. It means that I cooked over a fire, and took time to think, and that I slept in the woods and heard owls and coyotes in the night.

In full disclosure, I am making this particular smoky beard incident more idyllic than it was. This particular time I was leading a middle school camping retreat. Mostly it was burned hot dogs, no sleep, and lots of boys farting on command. One of those days I was climbing the rocks with a student on the west side of Devil's Lake. I was helping him get to the top—*Dude, I was helping him*—when he turned to me and said, "Can I help you make it up? My family is all about caring for old people."

I laughed and laughed. And he said, "It's funny, people always think I'm joking when I'm being serious. And they think I'm serious when I'm joking."

I was done laughing at this point, but he kept going, "Actually, I'm surprised that someone your age is even making this climb."

Thanks, kid. So much for my wild woodsman persona. In any case, this recognition of my smoky beard resonates with me because I want to carry around the aroma of exploits. Not for others to notice, so much, but as a reminder to myself. Like the rich, smoky, perfumed incense from that Eastern Orthodox chapel I go to sometimes on vacation. It gets in my clothes, and hair, and nose for days. It means I've experienced something more than myself, and my usual beaten path, and I don't want to stop thinking about that. About God.

And this second reason is related to the third. It's all I've ever really wanted to hear because it means I am known. That someone is in such proximity to me that she can smell campfire in my beard. More, it means I was kissed. It reminds me that I am a lucky man. Enveloped in blessings.

"Your beard smells like campfire." She said that to me. For real. Thank you, Jesus. Amen.

Aldo Leopold's Warning

Aldo Leopold, pioneering conservationist and Wisconsin icon, writes in his classic book *Sand County Almanac*, "There are two spiritual dangers in not owning a farm. One is the danger of supposing breakfast comes from the grocery, and the other that heat comes from the furnace."

Non-farmers and farmers alike, we tend to forget the source. I have a very bad memory. I forget how bad it is. Not long ago, my wife and I had our annual Talk. Maybe semi-annual, I can't remember. The Talk occurs when life has become busy and out-of-joint.

"It feels like we're living separate lives," she usually says. "Are you okay with this?"

There are tears, and she is right. Our jobs, which deal with lots of people, send us off in separate directions. Like we're in two rowboats, catching glimpses of the other only as the waves crest. "There! In the distance! Through the mist and spray!" Then we're dropped back into our respective troughs. Stroke by stroke, pulling away.

Our friend says she recently realized that she's been substituting her "work life" for her "real life." That somehow, home became peripheral. Her family had become a kind of support staff for her "real life"—her faux community of work.

We tend to forget the source. Leopold writes that the cures for these spiritual maladies associated with not owning a farm are to split a cord of wood or plant a garden. I imagine these would cause one to stop and consider the source. Probably all of my stunted spiritual growth can be attributed to the lack of stopping and considering. Like a skipping rock that flits across the surface of Lake Michigan, only pausing to take what it needs to stay above water. Frictionless living.

"All the fires that crackle here consume but do not burn. All light and no heat . . ." the dearly departed Mark Heard sang. And in that kind of consumer atmosphere—whether it be food, or heat, or family, or community, or even God Almighty himself—it all begins to look like it is here to serve me. That it all orbits around my gravity. I need no one. As Leopold observes, that is a great spiritual danger. The spiritual pioneer and icon Mother Teresa wrote, "Sometimes we must ask ourselves questions in order to inform our actions."

This is exactly what I don't want: for the skip of this stone to be interrupted with a question that would trip me, and drop me below the surface, into the depths. "Are you okay with this?" my wife asks. There's that sinking feeling. Now gasping for air. It is terrifying. But maybe drowning is good. Maybe I was just holding my breath anyway, waiting for the inevitable moment my disconnected life would begin to take on water. Maybe you have to go down in order to rise up for your real life. And questions, as I said, are usually the things that scrape a hole in the hull of my unanchored life:

Q: Where does this all come from? Not just food and heat, but love, and community, and breath, and me and . . . ?
Q: How does the way I am living my life right now affect others? From my wife and children, to my neighbor across the street, to my neighbor across the world? By commission or omission?
Q: What do I need to give? Or better yet: what do I need to receive? Bishop William Willimon wrote, "I suggest that we are better givers than getters, not because we are generous people, but because we are proud, arrogant people . . . It's tough to be on the receiving end of love, God's or anyone else's. It requires that we see our lives not as our possessions, but as gifts."
Q: What do I need to stop for God's sake? What do I need to start for my, and everyone else's, sake?

Whether farmers or not, we tend to forget the source. Are you okay with this?

Hunting for Words

As soon as I walked in, I knew something was wrong.

Blood was spattered at the entryway and then up each step. Large drops. More blood on the landing. Up the second flight. Through the second-floor fire door. And the trail stopped at room 201. I knocked nervously.

"Come in." And there he was, a bloody knife in his hand.

"What did you do, Rick?" I asked in disbelief. But it was obvious; his victim lay in plain view. Limp. Lifeless.

Who would've imagined, here in Stevens Point, Wisconsin? Right here in my college dorm. Actually, it wasn't too hard to believe. Rick was also the one who would hang upside down in his closet from gravity boots and wear shorts on the way to class when it was 20 below. It was only a matter of time.

"Why? How?" I stammered.

"It was easy," he explained, "I just opened the window and took my shot. Never saw it coming."

"A shot with what?"

"My blowgun," he said.

"What? You have a blowgun?"

"Yeh."

"You shot all the way from the second floor?"

"Yep," he said proudly.

"Nice shot," I exclaimed.

"Thanks. Yeah, I saw the rabbit in the bushes and nailed it with a dart." And Rick proceeded to skin that rabbit at his study desk. Right there in front of us in his dorm room. This was central Wisconsin. No big deal. He grew up hunting, like everyone else.

Well, except me.

I've never been hunting, which is probably fine. I like the idyllic picture of it, the way I like fishing—the solitude and the search. But my fear would be that I would actually shoot something. Or catch something: "Dear God, now what?"

In some ways, though, I think writing is like hunting. Or at least chasing rabbits in a thicket. I know some people say that the writing is "in them." They just have to dig it up. I'm not that confident in myself as a rich vein. I actually think that words are "out there." They are elusive and wild. It feels, for me, that they have to be hunted, called, tracked. Thus, I am in adulation when a word actually wanders into my sights. In deep thanksgiving when I can dress one on my desk. In awe when I can put a few together on my stringer.

"Yep. Just got back from a word hunt. Look at the size of this 900-word beauty. Had to land her with MS Word '98, but it made for a good fight. O' course I'm gonna have her mounted."

My Uncle Mike would be none too impressed; he gets 300-point bucks and 300-pound muskies every season. But in writing, as in hunting, you have to strike while the iron is hot. And in order to strike the hot iron, or whatever, you have to, well, check the temperature of the iron regularly, or however it works. I don't know. You gotta show up. Like Rick from his second-floor window. He was ready to strike, eyes peeled and blowgun at the ready. Or the guy in his underwear you always hear about, who shoots the buck from his kitchen window while he's drinking his coffee. Why does that guy keep his rifle right there next to the creamer? That was probably Rick, too.

But, last week, I jumped out of the shower 'cause I had to write something down for fear of losing it. I ended up forgetting to wash my hair. I probably wouldn't have to do that if I just showed up each day and wrote. I would catch more rabbits that way. Often, however, I don't have the wherewithal for the chase.

Actually, I am forcing myself to stay in this "word blind" right this very minute. Well, it's not really a duck blind or a tree stand. It's a chair at the Drink Coffee café in Sister Bay, Wisconsin. But I could bolt at any second and check my email. Or go to the bathroom. Or buy another coffee. Or check my email. Maybe I'm afraid of what I'll catch if I write too much, or the work of hauling it in. So I am envious of all my prolific writer friends who can churn out words daily. They are braver than I. It's said that the famous and prolific Wisconsin writer August Derleth could crank out 5,000 words a day—15,000 if he needed to. Courageous jerk.

Less a hunter, I am more like a driver hoping to hit a deer. Serendipitous, glorious roadkill. The prey, the capture, the gutting, the vehicle for delivery, all at the same place at the same time. Do you remember that story a few years ago, of the dozen or so white tails in Wisconsin that got on a highway overpass and ended up jumping over the guard rail? Head over hoof. Deer raining from above onto the interstate and the cars below. If only I were that lucky.

Indigenous Animals

Trillium. Dandelions. Indian paintbrush. Milkweed. Daisies. Queen Anne's lace. Black-eyed Susan. Jack-in the-pulpit. Purple coneflower. Cattails.

The average American can recall 1,000 brand names and logos, but can't name ten indigenous plants or animals. I read that somewhere. I think at a Starbucks.

Chipmunks. Thirteen-striped ground squirrels. Gray squirrels. Badgers. Juncos. White-tailed deer. Red-winged blackbirds. Red fox. Prairie chickens. Yellow perch. Bluegill. Mallards. Sandhill cranes.

I think these flora and fauna are all indigenous to Wisconsin. All off the top of my head. In fact, I can name two more: black-capped chickadees and moss. Chickadees were as common as gravel in Amherst, Wisconsin, where I spent part of my time growing up. And dark green moss was the carpeting in the white pine woods behind our house.

So, don't ask me why, but in fourth grade I snuck the BB gun out of our garage. My dad didn't want me playing with it, which is probably why I so wanted—needed—to do so. Anyway, I snuck the gun out to the backyard and headed off to the woods, where I spotted a chickadee in one of the pines.

Have you ever seen a black-capped chickadee up close? It's a common bird, but it is quite striking. Black velvet cap. A black bib. Deep black eyes. A luxurious gray waistcoat, with a downy white breast. And an infectious call from which it derives its name: *chik-a-dee-dee-dee*. Although it has every reason to be aloof and snobbish, it lingers and shows little apprehension. A gracious innocent among the arrogant, marauding blue jays and grosbeaks.

Don't ask me why I did it. At first I thought I missed. Dear God, I had hoped I'd missed. But never was a truer shot fired. Straight to its mark. All was quiet. Then, the bird fell over. Still gripping the branch. It swung. Underneath the branch. For a second. Then. Headlong to the moss below. A small, black and white form against the emerald floor.

I was horrified. Draped in guilt. Not for fear of getting in trouble for taking the BB gun out of the garage. That was a misdemeanor. The shock was from killing something beautiful, as much as a fourth-grader can understand that. Although, maybe fourth-graders have a better eye for beauty than others with 1,000 brand names stockpiled in their heads. I was horrified because there was no reason behind what I did. Maybe my first revelation that I had powder and shot packed inside my very own skin.

I didn't set out to shoot a chickadee. Even when I aimed and pulled the trigger, I was thinking I would just see how close I could get. But how does one measure that? Brinkmanship. I didn't mean to shoot the bird. Nor did I mean not to shoot it. Maybe that's the bigger crime. That was the source of my dread. Afterward, I stood over the chickadee, gun in hand, with what felt to be a rock on my chest.

Years later, one hunter friend told me he would place a berry in the beak of the quail and ring-necked pheasant he shot. Maybe even say a prayer. A Native American sign of respect, or something. I didn't have enough sense at the time. And the only prayer appropriate would have been one of repentance. All I did was leave the woods and sneak the gun back into the garage. I hid in my room. It wasn't until later, when I couldn't stand myself, that I confessed to my parents. I'm pretty sure I did that.

I can name a few wild things in my backyard today. But it was in fourth grade that I began to name the animals and weeds indigenous to my own heart.

Sasquatch

Now I lay me down to sleep. I pray the Lord my soul to keep. And if I die before I wake, I pray the Lord my soul to take. Amen.

This is a prayer we used to say as kids. I didn't remember it until my brother told me he had tried it out on his own boys one night recently. My ten-year-old nephew said he thought it was creepy. But I didn't remember thinking so back then, when I was six, or seven, or eight, lying under that blue and red plaid comforter. Life was dangerous as a kid, and there was no point in taking chances, even while sleeping. Especially while sleeping.

What could possibly be dangerous about being an elementary school kid in central Wisconsin? Plenty, in the 1970s. I am not talking about the danger that comes from falling out of pine trees, or from being run over by the family station wagon in the dead of winter, or from taking a garbage can lid and a tree branch, climbing onto your bike, and charging at your brother in a joust back there on George Street. I am talking about deeper mysteries that lurk on the edges. Sasquatch for one. Or Bigfoot, as he—it—was known to us rural white kids. Leaving only enormous foot prints, tufts of fur, grainy images and trembling children in his wake, what did that giant ape-like man want? Out there in the woods, watching?

My wife remembers praying to Jesus every night that Bigfoot would stay away. I am glad to report that God answers prayers.

There were other skulking menaces back then, too, like Great White sharks, piranhas, killer bees, UFOs, nuclear missiles. At any moment they could've snapped us up. Stripped our flesh. Swarmed us. Abducted us. Fallen out of the sky and laid waste to us. Any one of them. Or all at once. We shivered together as we watched the made-for-TV drama *The Day After*, and the impending nuclear winter.

All of these were lurking dangers, and I have not even mentioned the mysterious danger of liquid nitrogen. Some scientist in a lab coat came to Amherst Elementary School and poured an arctic liquid into a metal container, right there in the gym where we played dodgeball. Then, into that container, he slowly dipped a banana and then dropped it to the tiled floor. *Ta-daa!* It broke into smithereens like tropical glass. He told us never to touch liquid nitrogen. But what if we came across this inexplicable liquid on the side of the road? That's the information we really needed from that scientist. What if we accidentally touched it? What should we do then? Would it creep up our arms like ice from the back of the freezer and turn our flesh solid like petrified banana? Would we break into a million shards? Alone back there on George Street? It could happen.

Although the child's bedtime prayer was mysteriously creepy, it was an accurate depiction of reality. I was suspicious as a kid, and was pretty sure that life offered no happy endings. In my forties, I am convinced there are no happy endings. Life is a messier, more unpredictable muddle than we pretend. Recently, on Valentine's Day, in the Illinois community where I now live, a grad student opened fire in a university lecture hall. He shot 22 people. Six died, including the shooter. I told a friend, who had just gotten his master's from the school, that it was shocking: *Right here in our community.* He said he wasn't shocked. Sad, but not shocked. He was resigned to the fact that it would happen again. It was just a matter of time before it affected us.

We talk too much about happiness these days. Scientists in lab coats even study it. My research shows that we should save our breath and our grant money. Happiness is too easily stolen away by Bigfoot, missiles, and shotgun shells. To protect ourselves from cold, lurking devils we must cling to something else that is also below the surface. Something more mysterious. Something that extends past the dark woods. We must pray the Lord our soul to keep. Whether we wake or not.

Old Man Mix Tape

The Wintry Mix. The Roll Down Your Window Mix. Songs That Make You Say HYMN Mix. Music to Build a Deck by Mix.

I'm in a Seasonal Mix CD Swap. The mix CD is the offspring of the '80s mix tape. You still see some of these on the side of the road with their intestines spilled out.

I got asked by my friend Luke to be in this CD swap with nine other people. It's an honor because I'm 40 and everyone else is like 25. I'm not sure how I got in, but I must be pretty cool.

Here's how the Seasonal Mix CD Swap works: Every quarter—every season—of this past year, I've sent out a mix of songs I've been listening to, or that fits a theme, to nine other people. Mostly people I don't know. Mostly they're from Missouri. I live in Illinois. And then I have received nine CDs in the mail. That's like 180 songs. I suspected that since it was mostly Missourians that I would be getting 180 jug band songs a quarter, but that really hasn't been the case. It has been almost too much, though. I confess to just skimming through sometimes, but there are some real gems.

I'm glad to be in the Swap because, at my age, I've stopped looking for the flavor-of-the day bands, and my music options are dwindling. I am suspicious if the artist is under 30, so I don't bother. But the people I listen to are 50, maybe even 60 or 70. And several have even died. Johnny Cash most recently. But some lesser-known artists like Mark Heard and Gene Eugene, too. Of course, that means no more records from them. And no more music for me. So, it's good to have mixes from younger folks who are aware of younger, more diverse artists. And it's good for me to share some old man music, like T Bone Burnett, Lucinda Williams, Sam Phillips, Sister Rosetta Tharpe. And Mark Heard. Don't tell the rest of my Swap, but I feel like I'm bringing them culture.

This all sounds snotty, but I blame it on the mix tape era in which I was raised. It's easy to spit out a music mix these days. Just fire up iTunes, click a few boxes and then the "Burn CD" button. If one even bothers to make a CD anymore. But back in the day of cassettes you had to: 1) advance the tape past the lead (that short strip of white plastic that attached the tape to the reel); 2) hit the "record" and "pause" buttons at the same time on the tape deck; 3) set the recording levels; 4) drop the needle in the groove of the LP; then 5) quickly depress the "pause" button; 6) repeat 10 times; 7) pray to God the last song on Side A didn't go longer than the amount of tape left; and lastly 8) meticulously write out each song and artist on the 2" x 3" cassette insert. Next, turn the tape over. Repeat steps one through eight.

If you were gonna make a mix tape back in the day, it was serious business. A part time job. Giving someone a mix tape was a strategic move that meant you were gonna bring the musical hammer down on the recipient to show how cool you and your music were (and how much theirs sucked). Or, it was a move that meant you were infatuated with the recipient (like how in junior high I once sat and over-dubbed the name "Linda" 15 times into my cassette tape of the Billy Joel song "All for Leyna." It sounded something like this: "There's nothing else I can do/ 'Cause I'm doing it all for *clunk, screee,* [insert prepubescent 'Linda'], *screee, clunk;* I don't want anyone new/ 'Cause I'm living it all for *clunk, screee,* [insert pre-pubescent 'Linda'], *screee, clunk.*" Why I never captured Linda Barczewski's heart continues to be a mystery). So, of course, as a product of the '70s and '80s, I approached the CD mix swap as a competition. Subconsciously I desired to crush all others' attempts at music mixes. But I soon found that I carried around some scratchy LP attitudes in this clean, digital world.

The first CD mix I sent was a plain silver bullet with a list of tracks. Ka-blam! Bring it, Sucker. The nine discs I received, however, were pieces of artwork. There were handmade CD envelopes, some with original, playful illustrations. There were clever titles, like the "Daniel Boone vs. Abraham Lincoln Mix," the "Road Trip Mix," the "High-Low Mix," etc.

Silly youngsters. They'd get serious as soon as they heard my ultimate mix.

But the next quarter it was the same. Luke even made a CD mix of unorthodox renditions of hymns that included Andy Griffith and Faster Pussycat. He didn't care if it was mostly silliness. It was more of a communal experiment. I was shamed by their attitudes. My fellow swappers saw this as a community endeavor, not a battle of the bands like I did. They seemed to believe that they were sharing a piece of themselves, inviting me into their lives a bit.

One Swap member even emailed us all recently, "I've never met most of you guys, but I feel like I know you through the mixes. If it isn't too weird, it would be cool if we could all meet."

Well, it would be too weird for me, but isn't that what music is supposed to be—a medium that pulls people together? Somewhere I missed that, but I saw it clearly in the swap. As the year went on I couldn't wait to get the flood of CDs from Luke, Lisa, Jonathon, Jay, Tobie, Felicity, Christine, and Tom. I confess to even liking some of the bands they introduced me to, like G. Love & Special Sauce, Feist, Gogol Bordello, and Peter, Bjorn & Whoever. I even bought some of their songs.

In this year-long experiment I became a little less snobby about music. I did less skimming. Of course, my music is still superior to everyone else's, but I confess a warm appreciation and a slight infatuation for these nine mostly-strangers. I feel pretty cool to have been invited.

Baby, You're My Wisconsin

1.
Your kisses, like the waves at Little Sister Bay
Your bosom, like Devil's Lake, is where I lay
Your embrace: a squeeze 'tween Mendota & Monona
Who can even compare? They're full of Cudahy bologna

Chorus:
Summer, Autumn, Winter, Spring
Come around and begin again
Baby, you're my Wisconsin
Baby, you're my Wisconsin

2.
I don't mind it when you say, "You betcha"
Wanna wear just green & gold? Baby, I'll let ya
Your perfume of Leinie's, and cheese, and rivers
Fish frys, and pines, Darling, gives me the shivers
Chorus

3.
You're where Illinoisans can only visit and cry
Baby, you're where Canadians go when they die
Minnesota & Michigan: your homely sisters
If Indiana departed, Sugar, I wouldn't miss her
Chorus

Bridge:
Baby, this ain't no metaphor
(Darling, that's what poems are for)
Wisconsin, you're my Wisconsin

4.
Your kisses, like the waves at Little Sister Bay
Your bosom, like Devil's Lake, is where I lay
Your embrace: a squeeze 'tween Mendota & Monona
Who else can compare? They're full of Cudahy bologna

So, I wrote this song.

I had to. It's my job.

I'm from Wisconsin, but I've lived in Illinois the last 23 years. Thus, I am Resident Cheesehead, and Resident Packer Fan. The job descriptions for these positions are trash talk and smack talk, respectively. Except in summer, when Illinoisans call a truce and need to go on vacation in God's Country. Then I become tour guide: Where shall we go? Where shall we stay? Where shall we eat? How shall we converse with Wisconsinites? So this song is just part of the ongoing banter between me and my Illinois friends. And yes, I count them as friends, these neighbors.

This song was an assignment I gave myself. Usually, I write nonfiction. Essays. Some poems. But what would it be like to write a song? Specifically, a love song? The freedom to use all those terms of endearment, like Baby, Sugar, Darling. And the word bosom. Naturally, it became a song about Wisconsin. But a song needs more than lyrics; it needs music. I don't know the language of music, or the rules, so I put it out there on Facebook and on my website: "Win a $100 stack of cash! Set Kyle's 'Baby, You're My Wisconsin' poem/song to music! This means chords & a simple recording (MP3). Contest ends November 5, 2013."

There were lots of questions about how to pronounce Wisconsin names like Cudahy (CUD-uh-hay: a meat packing town near Milwaukee), and Mendota, and Monona (Men-DOH-tuh, Muh-NO-nuh: the lakes that squeeze the isthmus where Madison, the capital, is located), and Lienie's (LINE-eez: short for Leinenkugel's, a brewery in Chippewa Falls, Wisconsin). Part of me felt bad, because most of the people entering the contest were from Illinois. I felt like I was rubbing their noses in something. But, really, they were happily rubbing their own noses in it, which was cool to watch. One Illinois woman said, "I feel guilty singing this. Like my dad would disown me if he found out." But we're neighbors, and friends; we're all in on the joke. It's the good teasing that is not only okay, but important, in community. Even if it's a creative, digital community.

I lied when I said I had to write this song. I didn't. I just wanted to. And no one had to write music for the song, either. They just did it. The prize wasn't that big. But one woman restrung her autoharp for this. One high school girl got together with a friend from near the City and recorded it on a laptop, in a bathroom. A friend, who missed the contest deadline, called and gave a private concert with the song. A college student recorded multiple tracks. Someone recorded multiple versions. A married couple, late at night after putting their children down, created something from scratch. Together. All very busy people. Very busy.

It was much more than I expected. I was just looking for some simple chords to complete a song, but these were real-deal love songs. Guitars. Ukuleles. Mandolins. Violins. Accordions. A bass. A beer bottle as a slide. Percussion. Voices. Harmonies. The songs were sung and played with passion and seriousness. Now we were really in this together. Real collaboration with words and music coming together. I decided I couldn't judge them, so I sent the songs out to ten friends: Californians, Missourians, Wisconsinites, Illinoisans, Ohioans, Canadians. And these reviewers took their jobs seriously, too. Some went beyond just picking their top two songs and wrote full reviews! Here are some of them:

"Nice, downhome ukulele-accompanied-by-viola arrangement . . .. Makes me miss my childhood home in Wisconsin, and I grew up in Illinois!"

". . . like beautiful, aural feathers."

"Loved it. Made me think I was at a luau done Wisconsin-style: coconut bra slapped on over a parka."

"Fabulous. Catchy. Conveyed a wistful longing for Wisconsin . . . yet with a fun vibe. Didn't make me want to slit my wrists. The lyrics are campy and fun, so I felt the music . . . should echo that, without being weepy and eye-roll inducing."

"Jovial, energetic melody ambles along like a train. Great road companion—adding this to our 'road trip' playlist! Nice tambourine accompaniment."

"Warmhearted vocals and lovely accompaniment. This version feels like a . . . worship song to me. I wanted to wave my hands in the air, lift my closed eyes to the ceiling, and rock from side to side."

Even the reviewers built a connection around what was becoming a communal art project, rather than a contest. I started to feel like a hippie. A very clean hippie. But even more, I felt like I was part of a creative community. An arts community. I didn't even think of the song as mine anymore. I was reminded that encouraging others to be creative may be the most satisfying thing I do.

Why was this so satisfying for me? For us? Bottom line: it was Sabbath rest. Yeah, I said Sabbath. There were moments that felt like holy ground: How did they come up with this? Why are they taking time for this? It was enjoyable because we didn't have to do it. No one was looking to make a buck (the winner didn't even want the prize and gave it to charity), or to complete an assignment for a grade, or to strive in any way. It was like Sabbath because there was nothing we had to do, and we could do anything we wanted. It was playtime. A "snow day." A freebie. When's the last time I enjoyed that? When's the last time you enjoyed that? One guy even sent his song in after the deadline, 'cause he wanted to. We just played and shared together, to see what could happen. The individual results were wonderful and unique. The whole was even more intriguing. So I shared the reviews, and the results, and all the songs with the musicians.

This is what they said:

"I loved this."

"This is great! I loved hearing all of these."

"So. Fun."

"Let's do something like this again."

"Such a fun project. What's next?"

What's the next thing we can do together, indeed! They get it. One friend who entered said, "I'm going to have a contest where I write the music, and you have to write the lyrics about Illinois."

Yeah? Bring it. That's my dream job, neighbor.

Reading Room

I read that one edition of *The Wall Street Journal* has more information than one of the Pilgrims would have ingested in a lifetime. I'm not sure who figured that out, but I do know that after Thanksgiving turkey and stuffing at my mom's, my brother spent 30 minutes in the bathroom reading the *Stevens Point Journal.* He doesn't live in Stevens Point.

Much of my reading is done on the toilet these days. Out with the old, in with the new, like some bulimic librarian: Binge. Purge. Binge. Purge. The constant rolling flow of this microfiche brain. If I were ever to be alone with myself in my head, I'd probably pick up a magazine and pretend to read.

Gods of Fall

O gods of Fall, what have we done to offend thee? To deserve this? The low 70s and low humidity of early September have turned to muggy, upper 80s, boiling us in our own juices.

Was it the purchase of eggplant from the farmer's market, with big plans for parmigiana that, in the end, we let go to waste?

Was it the nights we chose television over campfires in the backyard?

Was it the Labor Day Weekend offense of not being present in that moment of sitting on the lawn, sharing a meal with dear friends?

We beseech thee, for this autumnal gluttony, sloth, and pride, forgive us.

For our thinking that everything lasts forever: Grant us mercy, and 45 percent relative humidity.

Amen.

Epic

The State Street Theatre marquee declares that *The Amazing Spider-Man* premieres tonight.

I was surprised at how thrilled I was this morning when I drove past. Confession: my dream life is that of Spider-Man. Is, not was. Was, and is. When I was in Mrs. Copps' class at Madison Elementary School, I would place Pink Pearl erasers around the hallways as "Spidey tracers"—Spider-Man's homing devices. I'd pretend to be Peter Parker with an eye out for danger. At 46, if I get a far-off look when I am talking to you, I'm probably thinking about what Spider-Man would do. Or, just about Spider-Man.

Every Saturday in elementary school, after digging through my mom's change purse—okay: after stealing from my mother—I would bike down to Gene's Grocery to buy the latest Marvel Comics issues. Thirty-five cents each. Then I'd sit in the woods behind our house, or in the attic space, and read those comics. "The Amazing Spider-Man" was and is my favorite, I think, because he was a smart-aleck who didn't have it all figured out, yet had some sense of responsibility with the power he was given. But mostly because he was a smart aleck with cool powers. Of course that's it.

Yesterday, a friend, whom I hadn't talked to in ten years, called and asked for prayer about a family crisis. His wife had just cheated on him for the second time in four years. They have several young children. He said, "You'll have to pardon me, but everything is so fucked up right now. I just wish for simpler times."

There was nothing to pardon. And, I prayed. And, he prayed. We shared some scripture passages for encouragement. His prayers were about healing for him and for her—stunning—and about justice, and about grace. And he could even joke a little bit in his dark moment.

After hearing my friend's struggle, and a bunch of other similar messes this week, like him I, too, wished for simpler times. Simpler times like escaping into the woods alone and just reading stories. But I think simpler times, with epic stories, serve to prepare us for increasingly dark times. Epic stories about people who don't have it all figured out, but want to be responsible, just, and gracious with their powers, and who can even be smart-alecky in the face of danger. I think my friend who wished for simpler times is drawing on his simpler times, and foundational, epic stories, to tell his own good story in the midst of despair. I think I was more encouraged by him than he was by me at the end of our phone call.

I plan to buy a pack of Pink Pearl erasers and go see a movie tonight.

New Vocab Word

I was passing through Lafayette, Indiana, with my family last week and noticed a statue of Marquis de Lafayette atop a fountain in the courthouse square. We stopped for a closer look after lunch. I don't know anything about Lafayette, except that he was a French general who aided Washington in the American Revolutionary War. On the statue's pedestal there is mention of John Purdue, founder of Purdue University. Truth be told, I believed the statue was the likeness of John Purdue until I sat down to write this a few days later and Googled it. Obviously, I don't know anything about John Purdue, either. And I don't know much about Indiana; I have a complicated relationship with the state.

But I'm not writing about Lafayette, or France, or Purdue, or Indiana. Rather, I was halted by a word inscribed under Purdue's name on the pedestal. A word I'd never heard before; I was surprised. I like to think of myself as having a decent vocabulary. A bit of a logophile (noun), if you will. I was, after all, runner-up in the school-wide spelling bee at Amherst Elementary in 1977. I was in fourth grade. I was beat out by a third grader over the word "chamois" (noun, of French origin; 1) a European mountain goat; 2) a type of pliable leather). FYI, it's not spelled s-h-a-m-m-y. Who knew? The third grader did. The Frenchman Lafayette probably did, too. I'm still embarrassed.

Anyway, the panel reads: "In Memory Of John Purdue Whose Munificence Gave Name To Purdue University." Again, this isn't about Purdue; it's about the monumental word that stopped me: the word "munificence."

"Munificence! What a word," we exclaimed. "Why have we never heard of it?"

Munificence (noun) is the quality or action of being lavishly generous. The word itself stands as a munificence. Above and beyond. A gift right here in Indiana. Who knew? Purdue's munificence was a gift of his personal wealth to have a university located in Lafayette, with the stipulation his name would be on it. Classes began at Purdue University in 1874, and the word munificence has not been heard much since the 1800s.

Munificence itself has been in short supply here in 2020. This is the year of the COVID-19 pandemic and of toilet paper hoarding, violent racial divisions, Right vs. Left, school and business shutdowns, social media barking and meanness.

A synonym of munificence is bountifulness. Bounty has the root of "goodness," something occurring in generous amounts. If anything, we have a bounty of division in 2020, but I think it's because we believe there is little goodness or abundance in the world. In this time we are afraid, believing the nature of the world is one of scarcity. We can't be gracious or merciful when it is Us vs. Them. We can't be munificent in that atmosphere.

Or can we?

Discovering the word munifice makes one want to be generous, and causes one to ask: *Whom do I know who is munificent? Am I munificent?* I had to go for a walk to think about this. To clear my head. The first presidential debate is later tonight—Trump vs. Biden—and my head is foggy with the stale vitriol (noun; cruel and bitter criticism; sulfuric acid) of social media.

Refreshed by autumn air, and under a moon pushing through the clouds, I began to make a list of people who are munificent. A list of friends who are givers, who always say *Yes* when a need arises.

My friend Ruth comes to mind. Ruth is a pie maker and, in my book, pie makers are lavish just by their existence. But more than just saying *Yes* when asked to help, Ruth is preemptive. She's on the lookout. She is the first on the scene with hospitality. If a family has a newborn, or sadly someone loses a baby, she brings meals. If someone is ill with COVID or recovering from surgery, she brings lasagna. She has some sixth sense, and is on the scene before you even know the need. She even gathers others to help serve.

Ruth, just so you know, is not retired with lots of time on her hands; she is a wife and mother with three young children, and she is a teacher. And, in 2020, the proof of her munificence to me is that she performs these acts of grace even toward those who would disagree with her on politics or doctrine. Her compassion is not diminished or withheld because someone is on the other side of the aisle. This is confounding to me and to those who would argue with her. Ruth, I think, would say that she can do this because she sees that God has made an abundant world. God has been gracious, and she can, in turn, pass that on to others without loss.

The culture around us, in this time, would tell a different story. A story of scarcity, and conservation, and reaction, and suspicion. I feel it in me. So I'm thankful for Ruth's reminder that we've been given a world of abundance, and thus we can live toward others out of that abundance—despite our differences.

And I'm thankful for this new vocabulary word.

Anthropology, Geology, Geography, Futurology

This morning I texted my daughter and son and told them, "I love you two."

My son texted back, "Love you, Pops!"

He's a senior in high school. I don't know when I became "Pops" to him. I like it. It feels intimate, and playful, and ascribes to me some sagacity. On the other hand, while writing this, I am remembering my great-grandfather, whom everyone referred to as Pop. I didn't know him at all. Just a few memories. He had buzzed white hair. Always a jacket and tie. Squinting, he sat silent in the corner at family gatherings with a cigar and a Schlitz. He was a relic. A bearskin rug. I gave Pop a wide berth out of respect, but I'm not sure why. Maybe that's what my son means when he calls me Pops. Yipes.

Later my daughter texted back, "Love you guys! Wish I could hang out with you today." And, to my surprise, I was almost in tears. She is a junior in college. I dropped her off for the start of the school year last week and felt the usual choking-up while saying good-bye to her and praying for her. Both the texts and the drop-off were surprisingly emotional, I think, because: 1) I really wanted to hang out with them; and, 2) because they are indicators of a shift. The initial shaky recordings of the seismograph. The shift is that soon—even now—my wife and I will not "hang out" with these two regularly. A week at Christmas. A week in the summer. My kids are not gone, but soon, and I miss them already. The geography of our little community is changing. It's spreading and becoming unfamiliar.

"Soon you two will be empty-nesters! How does that feel?" people are starting to ask my wife and me. The question usually comes from parents who are in the throes of potty training, or taxiing their middle schoolers to and from soccer: "Tell me—please, God— how does that feel?"

Confession: Along with sadness over my kids moving on, there is a slight concern that I, too, will become a relic. "Pops" as an anthropological find, rather than "Pops" as a growing, intentional presence. I don't know if my wife feels this concern. I need to ask her. A friend told me that once your kids are born, your dreams become about helping your kids achieve theirs. I get it; I love my kids. I want to help my kids. I love seeing them become the beautiful people they are, distinct from me and their mother. But, on the other hand, I'm not ready to discontinue having visions for my life, in part because it would be a disservice to my kids.

At this stage of life, the "second act" as my 70-year-old friend refers to it, these are some of the questions I am thinking about:

What is my purpose?
Who needs to be loved better?
What and where do I want to explore?
What do I want and need to learn?
What new things will I create?
What will be my legacy?

Of course, these are not new questions, and I have answers to some of them. But it's good to ask them again, now, so as to not become a relic, or lose a sense of geography. And yes, a large part of my "second act," I hope, will be "hanging out" with my kids and, God-willing, their kids. (I almost choked on my cigar and Schlitz while typing that.)

Creatures of the Northwoods

Wail-ail-ail! Honk-Onk-Onk-Onk! Whoop!

"What the devil?"

I am startled awake by this deep, echoing, trumpet sound right outside the Northwoods cabin, and I fumble for my glasses and phone. My gracious friends offered me their Land o' Lakes, Wisconsin, cabin for a writing retreat. I am here alone for the week—my wife agreed I couldn't pass up this gift—to write, to pray, to consider life in my "third act." I will be 52 in a few weeks and I have decisions to make about the future. The job I have does not have a long shelf life. And do people even hire 52-year-olds? Do I pursue a job possibility that has no guarantee? Do I strike out on my own?

At 1 a.m., on my first night, my heart is in my throat from this sonic blast. Maybe my future is more limited than I need to be worrying about.

Among my friends' instructions for the cabin: *consider bringing a can of bear spray.* As unsettling as that tip is, I can only wish this sound is that of a bear. It is unlike anything I have heard before. I check the windows. Nothing. A gibbous moon circled by clouds, the shimmering of Landing Lake, and the deep darkness of the pine and birch forest.

Again, the blast of a hoarse baritone, followed by what sounds like a dying car alarm, underscored by a sonar pulse. But none of it is mechanical. It is more prehistoric.

Again, it echoes across the lake. Calling. I am alone in the middle of the circling and soundings. I peer out the window and crack the sliding door slightly. A movement in the trees? Maybe. Then the sound of something thrashing the water. No one will believe this unless I can record it, so I hold the phone to the screen door for two minutes. Quiet. Then eight minutes. Nothing. Then ten minutes. Silence. The mystery continues; the creature doesn't reveal itself in response to my desire to identify it.

I go back to bed, Googling "creatures of Wisconsin forests," "animal sounds of the Northwoods," "I'm scared and alone up here," etc. Nothing helpful. I grew up with stories and folklore of mythical beasts in Wisconsin like Sasquatch, Hodag, Wendigo, Will-o'-the-Wisp, and Jack Pine. At 1 a.m. I am assembling a police line-up of creatures, but there is no one-way mirror between us.

I settle back to a troubled sleep.

2:30 a.m. Wail-*ail-ail! Honk-Onk-Onk-Onk! Whoop!* I jump out of bed, run to the door, and slide it open to record the creature. The calling is distant this time, across the lake, but I get 28 seconds of fuzzy audio. You hear it, don't you? That underlying, searching, sonar pulse element to it, right?

This creature, the Sounder of Landing Lake™ (as I've dubbed it, in case the newspapers want to talk to me, or I need to make t-shirts) is out there. I have seen it. With my mind's eye. I know what I heard. A figure, six feet tall—a conservative estimate—with a long pterodactyl beak (thus the resonance) lined with muskie-like teeth. A slender, long, tucked-in neck. And six long, avian limbs ending in webbed talons. Like a heron it steps cautiously through the shallows in the moonlight. #TheSounderOfLandingLake

Yet, the longer I listen in the dark: Is that a trumpeter swan in there? A common loon, too? Maybe a Canada goose, even? I see them all congregated in the bay near the cabin the next day. Dozens. An abundance of birds. All beautiful. And I get to experience them here.

Wail-ail-ail . . .

Honk-Onk-Onk-Onk . . .

Whoop . . .

Perhaps I am living my future now, in the sense that someone—my friend, God—was thoughtful and provided me this gift. A week surrounded by beauty and rest and creative endeavors. I did not expect it or predict it, and it's better than I could have imagined. I can trust it here and now. It is a gift. Why do I think that the future will be different? Not that the future will always be a restful retreat. But that it will be a gift. And beautiful. It has been to this point.

This unknowable creature with its mysterious calls does not seem so menacing to me anymore. In fact, I fall asleep to the distant echoing beauty. In the end, I think it is heralding something out there. What? I don't know. A far-off companion? Its Maker? An abundant life?

I place a personal ad in the *Vilas County News-Review*: Dear Sounder of Landing Lake, Despite my initial terror, I hope you are out there. Maybe you hope I'm out there, too. Maybe we could even be friends. Kind Regards, KLW

In Advance

I just sat down in my garage, on that red leather chair. How it made its way into the garage—or more, why it stayed there—I can't recall. It was put into retirement. Old and cracked.

I have been cleaning out the garage for several hours, to create some order. It is Saturday, midday. There is a pile of dust, bent nails, and scraps in the middle of the cement floor. Half-full garbage bags. Some boxes over there. A broom leaning against a table over here.

In that chair I begin to fall asleep, then am surprised by the thought: This may be how I die someday. Dozing off, legs crossed, head drooping to my left shoulder, arms resting on the arms of the chair. It may be. Hopefully not in these shoes I use for mowing, or in this shirt. But I definitely will die with a pile of unfinished work. Things out of order. As much as I try to organize and tuck things away, or sweep them under rugs, there will be a mess in the middle of the floor, and one you'll find later in the corner. A mess you'll have to clean up. I am sorry. I wasn't expecting this on a Saturday, midday.

I recall a bit of a prayer from a recent funeral: "May we all miss him deeply, and forgive him often . . ." In light of the mess to come, the mess yet to be revealed, I ask you to forgive me. In advance. And every time thereafter that you think of me. Just don't think of me in these shoes, and in this shirt.

Wendell Planted a Tree for Me

Wendell planted a tree for me.

When I resigned from a local church where I worked with middle- and high-school students, Wendell, a humble history teacher and devoted gardener, planted a tree in the garden out front of the church. He said it was as a remembrance for my work there. Wendell passed away a few years ago, and I drive past his house on Somonauk Road everyday and think it's sad that some people don't know or remember him. His wife Ruth slipped into Alzheimer's about ten years before Wendell died. She didn't remember him, but he would visit her in the care facility every day for lunch, for years, and care for her.

Anyway, after a dozen years or so, I returned to staff at that same church, and at some point I noticed that the tribute tree was no longer there. It got chopped down! My memorial tree was chopped down. Not at the hand of some malicious rival, I don't think. Maybe the tree didn't survive. Or maybe someone cut it down to make way for some new gardening activity. The church as an organization of revolving volunteers has mostly short-term memory.

At first I thought about the loss of the tree: *That's disappointing.* Sad, even. I don't think I was offended. But now I laugh every time I pull into the church parking lot and pass the garden and that empty, tree-shaped space.

It is a daily reminder that I am not indispensable. That I will one day be bygone. Obsolete. Obsolete means "no longer of use."

My friend Ron from church once told me, "In 20 years, unless you're Eisenhower or somebody, no one will remember you."

"You mean Bill Eisenhower?" I was tempted to ask.

At first Ron's thought felt disheartening: *What about all my important work? These relationships? That clever thing I said that one time?*

It is in part why I write. I want my story to live on. I want my kids to remember. And so on.

But no one is asking, "Hey, what happened to that tree?" It will be the same with me at some point. In the end, the tree and I are dispensable.

Rather than disheartening, I find the idea of obsolescence a relief. It's what I want from any vacation. At some point I will no longer need to carry some perceived monumental load. The load of looking busy. Of self-importance. The delusional load that I am the main character around which all others act. That if I don't show up, things won't get done. Obsolescence, then, is restful. It's Sabbath. It's reality.

I want to practice obsolescence now. Practice living in reality.

And, in one particular way, I do.

Once a month, in our church, we partake of communion. We share bread and Welch's grape juice (the grape juice is in remembrance of Prohibition). We share it that morning in remembrance of the Suffering Servant and his coming again. Present, past, and future reality all in one beautiful, mundane celebration. It reminds me that mine is not the life-giving story to be lifted up. Recently, we began serving gluten-free bread at one of the communion stations. My friend Lowell, a farmer from Indiana, and another humble gardener, was the first one to serve up front at that station. Our pastor explained the gluten-free bread option. I was seated near the front of the church, and Lowell and I locked eyes. He made a Midwest shrug in my direction, nonplussed, as if to say, "I don't know what this is all about, but okey-doke. It's fine. I'm just glad to be here."

The older I get, the more I want to be like Wendell and Lowell. Those humble saints. In the collective memory of the church, mine is not the remembrance story. Nor is yours. I need to remember that. We need to remember that. The missing tree is a good reminder.

This should be a proverb, or at least a fortune cookie message: *Your tree of remembrance shall become the stump of obsolescence. And that's a good thing. It's fine. Your lucky numbers are 5, 11, 19, and 67.* Amen.

Winter, No. 1

In late fall, my wife takes a sickle and cuts all her garden flowers to the ground. She says it's to make room for new growth in the spring. The mown plants now look like dark, broken pipes jutting from the snow. Desolate. Stark. Sorrowful.

I admire my wife's patience for growth. She sees through winter's hollow darkness to blooms of coneflower, bee balm, daisies, sedum, lilies, coreopsis, bleeding heart, and obedient plant.

Notes

Freezing, Thawing: New & Revised Stories from the Midwest has new stories, and ones previously published in the books *Wisconsin River of Grace* (Cornerstone Press, 2009), *Neighbor As Yourself* (2016), and *Winter Is Scissors* (2018). Why revised? A priest, a minister, and a rabbit walk into a bar. The rabbit says, "I think I might be a typo."

"Speeds Bumps for Glaciers," p. 35

So, in June of 2015, I was at my doctor's office to get some shots for some out-of-country travelling I'd be doing. I couldn't remember the last time I needed a shot. As the nurse swiped the cotton ball on my upper arm, the smell of rubbing alcohol sent me immediately back in time to Dr. Sevenich's office. Dr. Sevenich was my childhood doctor. Everything in his office and exam room was antiseptic and orderly. Silver syringes neatly lined up on a tray. I remember his white physician's smock, his neat mustache, and the glass jars of cotton balls, tongue depressors, and Saf-T-Pop suckers. Brewers on the office radio. He was great with kids.

He sticks out in my mind, probably because he was kind, and because he was present for traumatic situations like stitches and shots. And for the time my mother ran me over with her car. Dr. Sevenich even shows up in the essay "Speed Bumps for Glaciers" (originally in my book *Wisconsin River of Grace*). It's all about the wounds I received at the hand of Wisconsin's geography and geology. And how scars are good reminders. The closing line of that essay is this: ". . . no need to call Dr. Sevenich, God rest his soul, I get it now."

So, after being transported back in time to his office via isopropyl alcohol last year, I Googled: "James Sevenich MD Stevens Point Wisconsin." Not sure why. Memory Lane. It's what we do. The search showed the honors he had received, his bowling scores, etcetera. But the 11th hit surprised me by linking me to an essay I had published, in a Wisconsin arts paper, back in 2010. There was a comment on that essay that I never saw before. Here's what it said: "Hey Kyle. Just read your book, *Wisconsin River of Grace*, and really enjoyed it. Note pages seven and nine. I'm still alive and kicking. Sincerely, James R Sevenich M.D., Stevens Point, WI." What?! I couldn't stop laughing! And I still can't! I knew he was good, but was he that great a physician that he healed himself? Dr. Sevenich back from the dead? No, it was my mistake.

In all the book publisher's fact checking, and obtaining permissions, it didn't occur to us to check if someone was actually dead or alive. That's a bigger problem if you're a physician than if you're a writer, but still. Honestly, I thought I got it from a pretty good source that he had passed away. Maybe my dad, or my aunt? I dunno. There's more to talk about here, but, in the end, two questions: What was it like for Dr. Sevenich to read of his demise in a book he purchased? And, what was it like for him to give such a gracious response? Dr. Sevenich, God bless your soul.

People said I should contact him. I never got around to it. Well, in March of 2016, I received a message on social media that said this: "It is with regret and a heavy heart that I inform you Dr. Sevenich has passed this last Saturday." It was from Dr. Sevenich's son. On Monday. So, we started a conversation online. I offered my condolences and he replied: "We oscillate wildly right now between joy of being part of his life and sorrow in his passing. So many wonderful memories."

His son shared photos of journal entries from his dad. They figured he delivered just over 4,000 babies in his career. I was one of them. He showed me the ledger entry from my birth in 1967. But why would he contact me? And just a day or so after his father's passing. I hadn't seen Dr. Sevenich in over 30 years. I never met his family. His son explained: "My father has a copy of the book signed by you. He highlighted the references to him; he was so delighted."

Why did Dr. Sevenich's son contact me? Because the reference and inaccuracy in my little book became a delight to his gracious, funny father. The act of remembering—and writing is the act of remembering—can be a sign of affection. Even when you don't realize it. So remember often, and speak your affections broadly.

"Significant," p. 76
I was asked to read this at my friends' wedding. It was the first wedding I attended in the pandemic. Matt and Brenda pared their celebration down and made it lovely. But I have felt badly for all, in this pandemic, who have had to reduce or postpone celebrations, like graduations,

weddings, anniversary trips, etc. I have loved seeing all the creativity and resilience in this time.

"This Is Practice," p. 81

Jesus says: "Are not two sparrows sold for a penny? And not one of them will fall to the ground apart from your Father. But even the hairs of your head are all numbered. Fear not, therefore; you are of more value than many sparrows." (Matthew 10:29–31)

The word that keeps coming to me during COVID-19 has been "humility." I am not in control. I don't understand or know everything. In fact, very little, despite my certainty on social media. I am not as safe and sound as I make myself out to be. I am more impatient than I pretend, more fearful, with less stamina. Yet I am more seen by God, I am more preened over—he counts the number of hairs on my graying head—and I am more valued than I imagine. In one of Kierkegaard's journals he writes: "Not a sparrow shall fall on the ground without your Father: then all at once I felt how great and small I was; then did those two mighty forces . . . happily unite in friendship." I read this in Kathleen Norris' *Acedia & Me: A Marriage, Monks, and A Writer's Life*. This book was my guide through the initial lockdown of the pandemic. I plan to return to this book often.

By the way, my dad is doing much better.

"I'll Never Go Back to that Library," p. 84

The Innocence Mission carried me through the beginning of the pandemic. Poetic, restful, reflective. If you are new to them, try songs like: "Bright As Yellow," "North American Field Song," "On Your Side," "Lakes of Canada," and "Green Bus."

"Look at This, Neighbor," p. 85

Once again, Jesus says: "Are not two sparrows sold for a penny? And not one of them will fall to the ground apart from your Father. But even the hairs of your head are all numbered. Fear not, therefore; you are of more value than many sparrows." (Matthew 10:29–31)

Also, in this renewed sense of humility brought on by COVID-19, I have become more aware that my neighbors are afraid, that they could fall to the ground any minute, too. In fact, many of my neighbors are in more suspense than I am. I think of beautiful Haiti (consider supporting this children's home and school in Mirebalais, Haiti—it is near and dear to me: gracesoamazingministries.org), racked with poverty and modern-day slavery, and now COVID-19. I think of my low-income friend of color who said, when I asked if he was worried about coronavirus, "It's not the first thing I'm worried about." In our mutual uncertainty, the very least I can do in the name of Christ is to let my neighbors know they are seen, cared for, and valued by me.

Makoto Fujimura's book *Culture Care: Reconnecting with Beauty for Our Common Life*, which I quoted here, is taking me new places. Consider reading it in these divisive times.

"Baby, You're My Wisconsin," p. 106
Listen to the entries from the song contest here: https://bit.ly/3jZWy6p
I would love to hear your version, too!

Made in the USA
Columbia, SC
26 June 2021